A PLUME BOOK

EMOTIONAL CHAOS TO CLARITY

PHILLIP MOFFITT is currently director of the Life Balance Institute, co-guiding teacher of Spirit Rock Meditation Center, and guiding teacher of Marin Sangha in San Rafael, California. He is also the author of *Dancing with Life: Buddhist Insights for Finding Meaning and Joy in the Face of Suffering*.

Praise for *Emotional Chaos to Clarity*

"*Emotional Chaos to Clarity* is a masterwork. Be inspired by the possibilities it opens. Be strengthened by the guidance it offers in decision making. Be surprised by the illumination that comes when you contrast your ideals with your actual days. And be encouraged in the midst of your life challenges by the power and love that comes when you see and live by your highest intentions."

—Jack Kornfield, PhD, author of
The Wise Heart and *A Path with Heart*

"Phillip Moffitt takes the profound insights of the wisdom traditions and translates them into simple and effective steps to stable inner strength, happiness, and peace. His unique gift is his own deep grounding in what it really takes to be fully engaged with life while remaining clearheaded and happy. An extraordinary book."

—Rick Hanson, PhD, author of *Buddha's Brain:
The Practical Neuroscience of Happiness, Love, and Wisdom*

D0964887

"Building on a history of finding his way out of a meaningless, albeit successful, worldly life into a life of service, Phillip Moffitt has crafted a highly practical handbook for navigating the inevitable challenges that beset us. A marvelous tool to have handy when our better knowing is overwhelmed by those often mysterious interior storms, this book communicates a desperately needed feeling that we can indeed succeed in shaping lives of meaning."

—Don Hanlon Johnson, PhD, author of
Everyday Hopes, Utopian Dreams: Reflections on American Ideals

"In *Emotional Chaos to Clarity*, Phillip Moffitt maps out a path for opening and expanding our sense of what is possible, what we are capable of, what will bring us true happiness. He also shows us step-by-step how to apply acceptance, kindness, awareness, and compassion in order to make those aspirations come to life. To move from emotional chaos to clarity is not a minor journey, but it is possible, and for any one of us, it can be real."

—Sharon Salzberg, author of *Loving-Kindness* and *Real Happiness*

"Phillip Moffitt presents a clear path to living an authentic and intentional life. He has a profound understanding of how emotions distort our perceptions and how we can create new, healthy habits of mind."

—Dean Ornish, MD, author of *The Spectrum*

Emotional Chaos
to Clarity

*Move from the Chaos of the
Reactive Mind to the Clarity of the
Responsive Mind*

Phillip Moffitt

A PLUME BOOK

PLUME
Published by the Penguin Group
Penguin Group (USA) Inc., 375 Hudson Street,
New York, New York 10014, USA

USA | Canada | UK | Ireland | Australia | New Zealand | India | South Africa | China
Penguin Books Ltd, Registered Offices: 80 Strand, London WC2R 0RL, England
For more information about the Penguin Group visit penguin.com

First published in the United States of America by Hudson Street Press, a member of Penguin
Group (USA) Inc., 2012
First Plume Printing, 2013

P REGISTERED TRADEMARK—MARCA REGISTRADA

THE LIBRARY OF CONGRESS HAS CATALOGED THE HUDSON STREET PRESS EDITION AS FOLLOWS:

Moffitt, Phillip.
Emotional chaos to clarity : how to live more skillfully, make better decisions, and find purpose
in life / Phillip Moffitt.
p. cm.
Includes index.
ISBN 978-1-59463-092-7 (hc.)
ISBN 978-0-14-219676-2 (pbk.)
1. Emotions. 2. Life skills. 3. Self-actualization (Psychology) I. Title.
BF531.M64 2012
152.4—dc23 2011046151

Printed in the United States of America
10 9 8 7 6 5 4 3

Set in Granjon LT Std

While the author has made every effort to provide accurate telephone numbers, Internet
addresses, and other contact information at the time of publication, neither the publisher nor the
author assumes any responsibility for errors or for changes that occur after publication. Further,
publisher does not have any control over and does not assume any responsibility for author or
third-party Web sites or their content.

DEDICATION

Dr. Joseph L. Henderson, M.D. (1903–2007), author, psychiatrist, and Jungian analyst.

"Joe" was my analyst first, then my mentor, and finally my friend. Over a twenty-year period, he led me through understanding the subtle mysteries of the archetypes in the unconscious, the role symbols play in the psyche, how dreams can be interpreted, and the vital need for initiation in each stage of our lives. Working until he was 102, Joe helped many individuals journey from emotional chaos to clarity.

CONTENTS

PART III: Removing the Sources of Chaos

ACKNOWLEDGMENTS

I want to express my appreciation to Caroline Sutton, my editor at Hudson Street Press, for her enthusiasm for this book and to Stephanie Tade, my agent, for finding the perfect home for it.

I also want to acknowledge my teaching colleagues at Spirit Rock Insight Meditation Center and Insight Meditation Society, who collectively offer the wisdom of the Buddha's teachings to all who are interested. Many thanks to Jack Kornfield, who gave generously of his time to review my manuscript.

I am grateful to my meditation students, particularly the members of the Marin Sangha, whose questions and comments helped shape many of these teachings. I also appreciate the courage and generosity of my Life Balance clients who have allowed me to share their stories and hard-won insights.

I'd also like to thank my partner, Pawan Bareja, for her patience while I spent long hours writing on most weekends and for forgoing all but one week of vacation until the book was complete.

I want to credit my dear friend David V. White, who has contributed in countless ways to my understanding of how to gain clarity. We have been fellow travelers on the journey of insight for more than forty years. During a time when I was living in New York City and struggling with my own emotional chaos, David flew to the city and spent a weekend reading T. S. Eliot's *Four Quartets* out loud to me. It was the first time I realized the deep wisdom with which Eliot addressed the modern dilemma of suffering, and Eliot's words continued to be of great comfort to me during that difficult period.

What I most need to acknowledge are the diverse, multiple, and invaluable contributions of Kathryn Arnold, the creative director of the Life Balance Institute. When she was editor in chief of *Yoga Journal*, Kathryn got me to start writing about skillful living in my Dharma Wisdom column. Now, as my colleague at the institute, she is the one who waded through four hundred different talks I've given and numerous articles I've written and suggested the initial outline for *Emotional Chaos to Clarity*. Kathryn then worked with me every step of the way to create the manuscript. This book simply would not exist without her efforts. Thank you, Kathryn.

A NOTE ON THE COVER

I chose the shell of the chambered nautilus for the cover of this book because it symbolizes the spiral-like growth that the human psyche undergoes in journeying from chaos to clarity.

This enduring sea creature, which has existed for 500 million years, lives in an exquisite shell that is a perfect logarithmic spiral. The creature grows continually and, as it does, it seals off the chamber it inhabited previously and lives in the outermost chamber of its shell. Similarly, our search for clarity is a continual process of growth and requires that we be willing to live at the outermost edge of our awareness.

Unfortunately, the chambered nautilus is now in danger of extinction due to commercial exploitation. If you would like to help preserve this ancient creature, please consider refraining from purchasing any jewelry or other decorative objects made with their shells.

INTRODUCTION

From Emotional Chaos to Clarity

Let's be honest. Isn't it true that no matter how hard you try to make your life the way you'd like it to be, it's still difficult, disappointing, and stressful at times? Life just doesn't always go the way you'd planned or hoped. Consequently, isn't it also true that your mind is often in turmoil? In addition to all the anxiety created by thinking, planning, and making the decisions that go into fulfilling your dreams and goals, you are beset by uncertainty about how things will turn out. Your confusion is compounded by the tension that arises when your wants and needs conflict with those of others. I call this mental storm *the emotional chaos of the untrained mind.*

Emotional chaos is the result of *reactive mind states*. You know all too well what these are: anger, anxiety, frustration, irritation, restlessness, worry, insecurity, doubt, obsession. They can stem from a relationship problem (with a family member, friend, or romantic partner), a challenging work situation, a health issue, or some personal limitation. The reactive mind is like a puppet on a string being pulled first one way and then another by its perception of how things are going. When it likes what is happening or might happen, it is automatically pulled toward wanting to keep what it perceives as pleasant; when it dislikes what has happened or may happen, it pushes away the unpleasantness. The chaos that arises from this constant pushing and pulling drains your energy and affects your mood, causing you to lose perspective. Therefore you find it harder to maintain a sense of well-being, even when your life is going just fine. You often act and speak unskillfully or are bombarded by unwholesome thoughts. Your life deteriorates into melodrama, and you become stuck in a soap opera of your life. Do you really want to live like a puppet on the end of your emotional strings?

Discovering the Clarity of Responsive Mind States

These reactive mind states are not really your fault. Life is unpredictable and sometimes painful, so of course it generates mental and emotional chaos. But you do not have to be a passive victim of this barrage of thoughts and feelings; you do not have to helplessly submit to your mind being tossed around willy-nilly by these inner storms. There is a way to move from the emotional chaos of the reactive mind to a state of clarity in which you are able to respond to people and situations from a *responsive mind state.* Your responsive mind *knows what you are about.* It allows you to stay grounded in your deepest values even in the face of life's uncertainty. The responsive mind isn't swayed from its larger purpose merely because you intensely desire or dislike someone or are having a bad day. You may not like what is happening in an interaction or situation—you may even be very unhappy about it—but when you are living from your responsive mind, you will not get lost in your displeasure and react in a manner that isn't reflective of your genuine self. You experience clarity that allows you to act with wisdom and stay true to what matters most to you. This abiding wisdom yields a sense of ease and direction in life that I call *skillful living.* Although you can't make your life perfect, you can, without question, learn to live more skillfully. The result is that you begin to feel as though you have choices regarding both what you do and how you feel about what happens to you. It is a deeply satisfying experience to feel that your life is authentically your own.

You already have moments when you are living from your responsive mind; if that weren't true, you would fall into permanent dysfunction, depression, and/or nihilism. But how fully you live from that capacity, and how quickly you regain it when you get caught in emotional chaos, is where skillful living makes all the difference. The combined skills of *mindfulness* and *intention* described in this book represent an approach to transforming life's many challenges into opportunities for growth. This approach constitutes the foundation for a more authentic relationship with yourself and others. As you apply these life skills you will feel more grounded and oriented in your life. My purpose in writing this book is to assist you in this process of learning how to live more skillfully.

Imagine living without feeling as though your life were a soap opera. Imagine abandoning your expectations about what your life should be like and awakening to a deeper, more meaningful and satisfying relationship with your life just as it is. Imagine feeling empowered to move toward your goals without fear, worry, emotional contraction, or a grasping mind state that is always creating stress. More specifically, here are some of the benefits of skillful living that this book seeks to help you discover:

- You know and act from your core values at all times.
- You gain wisdom from both pleasant and unpleasant experiences.
- You can discern between thoughts, words, and actions that cause harm and those that do not, and you act accordingly.
- You know your true nature, the essence of your character, and how to protect it.

- You accept gain and loss equally and derive insight from each.
- You have an inner life in which love can flourish, even if your outer life is filled with challenges.
- You learn to speak only what it true, useful, and timely, even during moments of anger and outrage.
- You are not controlled by your views and opinions or the story of your past, but rather you have a "don't know" mind that responds wisely to whatever you encounter in life.
- You have the ability to soothe yourself whenever you feel disappointed or overwhelmed by life.

My Own Journey toward Skillful Living

I write with such confidence about the possibility of changing your life, of moving from emotional chaos to clarity through mindfulness and wise intention, because of the dramatic changes I have made in my own life, and because I have worked with thousands of individuals and seen for myself that we do not have to stay imprisoned by our reactive mind.

I began to focus on intention, authenticity, and skillful living when I was thirty-four years old. I was editor in chief and CEO of *Esquire* magazine and had enjoyed great success. But my life seemed out of balance. I felt as though I wasn't living from my authentic self. Even though my external life was fun and stimulating, my internal experience was that of not being connected to a larger purpose.

I'd launched my first magazine when I was twenty-two and became accomplished at conceiving new ideas for magazines, editing them, and making money in the process, but with each passing year I felt more and more as though I was just repeating what I had already done and not really growing or discovering new capacities within myself. Although I became increasingly successful, I wondered to what end. I did not value money or glory sufficiently to justify living without feeling that I was doing what mattered most to me. I was grateful for the worldly gains I had achieved, but their value steadily diminished as I acquired more of them, and the effort required to keep succeeding in the same way felt like a grind.

After much debate with myself, I abruptly left *Esquire*, when I was forty, to explore the inner life. Naturally, my friends and colleagues in the publishing world thought this was a bizarre decision. It seemed strange to me too! Yet it also felt invigoratingly authentic. After leaving *Esquire*, I spent many years without any clear direction in my life. All I knew was that I must not fall into the trap of seeking worldly accomplishment as an end in itself.

I moved from New York to California; spent many months each year doing long, silent meditation retreats; underwent Jungian analysis; studied the relationship between body and mind; earned a black belt in aikido; and started a nonprofit life-skills-training organization called the Life Balance Institute, which helps people find direction and meaning in their lives and develop the kind of life skills taught in this book. Eventually I began to offer meditation retreats. I have taught and worked with thousands of meditation students, some of them in one-on-one relationships over many years. I've also trained other meditation teachers, as well as psychotherapists. I've taught seminars in sustainable leadership to CEOs and counseled hundreds of entrepreneurs and leaders during major life transitions. I have taught self-care to care providers and mindfulness to people in prison. This book owes a debt of gratitude to all of these individuals. Their lives were the laboratory for discovering what genuinely creates a skillful life. I offer some of their struggles and successes as examples throughout this book. To protect their privacy I have changed their names, and in some cases the details of their lives.

I will tell you the same thing I tell my Life Balance clients: I am not a psychotherapist; I am an *interventionist*. I intervene because I want to help you strategize about your life and create a plan. I want you to take your inner life more seriously and to understand how misleading surface appearances can be, because I want to help you discover more meaning and well-being in your life. This book is not a psychological exploration of how life skills become limited during one's development but rather a series of insights and practical understandings that can help you bring change and balance to your life in this moment, with you being just as you are.

How This Book Is Organized

As you will discover, *Emotional Chaos to Clarity* is not theoretical but rather pragmatic and immediately applicable. It is intended to be an inspiration and reminder of what matters most, as well as a practical guide for navigating through confusion, disappointment, and tough decision making.

It is a book of wisdom based on the hard-earned knowledge of many people who have committed to being present in their lives.

The book is divided into three parts. The first, "Practices That Empower You to Achieve Clarity," explores what it means to be human and helps you reconnect to what matters most to you. The chapters in this section help you create a vision of who you would be if you lived with clarity and provide the foundation you need to fully utilize the practice-specific chapters in the next two sections. The second part, "Developing Skillful Behaviors," presents the skills you need to bring clarity into your life. These chapters focus on developing wholesome goals and skillful means that enable you to meet life more effectively and authentically. The third part, "Removing the Sources of Chaos," examines the reasons why people behave unskillfully at times and cause suffering for themselves or others. The chapters in this section help you hurdle the roadblocks on the journey away from habitual chaos and live from the clarity you have gained.

Every chapter is followed by a self-assessment exercise, a set of practices, or a reflection, to help deepen your understanding of the insights it offers. You'll notice that I deliberately repeat certain practices throughout the book. I do this because scientific studies have revealed that we learn best when we are exposed to new information in a variety of contexts. I also want to show you how the wisdom gained from reading this book can be applied across various aspects of your life.

Realizing the Imaginative Possible

I call the moment when you fully know that a change is achievable *realizing the imaginative possible*. When you are able to envision that an alternative is real, you experience a sudden energetic surge toward actualizing it, which becomes self-reinforcing. Previously you may have wanted to make a change, and maybe even worked hard at it, but you never truly believed it was possible. Now, though you are still not certain you *can* do it, you know it is a genuine possibility. You suddenly have confidence that the change you desire is achievable.

When you lack confidence, you are less likely to trust your intuition and act boldly. Moreover, you give mixed signals to others about your capability and commitment. With the realization of the imaginative possible, all these limitations disappear. It's as though the brain is recalibrated in a manner that significantly increases the likelihood that the desired change will occur. This experience can arise through insight or through opening the heart. It is a palpable feeling of something in you being significantly different, and if you are mindful, you will feel it. It is one of the most powerful tools I have encountered for gaining a sense of choice in life.

The practices outlined in this book open the way to encountering such moments. If such a moment arises for you—a moment when you realize that it is genuinely possible for you to live more skillfully in some aspect of your life and that you have choices you never before recognized—I suggest you take time to allow your mind to settle into it, so you can begin to embody this new possibility. I feel honored to accompany you on this inner exploration of discovering what is possible for you.

May your efforts bring you a calm, clear mind and a peaceful, loving heart.

Phillip Moffitt
Marin County, California
April 2012

Part I

Practices That Empower You to Achieve Clarity

The most challenging mental habits to break free of are your misperceptions about who you are. The first chapter in this section introduces the concept of *mindfulness*, which forms the foundation on which we will build. Chapter 2 examines the tendency we all have to misapprehend how identity is created and the chaos that this confusion causes in our lives. Once you understand how you may be imprisoned by mistaken beliefs about your identity, you can open up to new possibilities for living more authentically.

It's not easy to achieve clarity about who you are or what genuinely matters to you. However, there are four fundamental practices that can empower you as you make this journey. The first of these practices is *setting intentions* based on your core values. When you are clear about your values and know your intentions, you can respond skillfully to the events in your life rather than react impulsively. Chapter 3 explores the benefits of living from your intentions and how to do so.

Chapter 4 introduces you to the practice of *starting over* when you become lost on your journey from emotional chaos to clarity. There will be moments when you forget your intentions and act unwisely, so it's essential that you develop the ability to just start over; otherwise you may become discouraged and give up.

The third practice is *letting go of expectations*, which can undermine your intentions. Chapter 5 reveals how hidden expectations can become all-powerful and cause you to act unskillfully, and it explains how to free yourself from the tyranny of expectations.

Chapter 6 presents the fourth practice, *balancing your priorities*, which helps you align your allocation of time, energy, and resources with your intentions. When you're in conflict about what to do in a situation, clarity about your priorities can help you make the right decision.

Incorporating these four practices, along with mindfulness, into your daily life creates the foundation for understanding your true nature and for living skillfully. Each of these practices will yield immediate benefits in your life; collectively they allow you to journey into a deep exploration of what really matters to you.

Chapter 1

Beginning Your Journey to Clarity

If you are motivated to bring more clarity to the chaos of your mind, it is crucial that you have some kind of practice for staying present and aware during its moment-to-moment movement. Mindfulness meditation, the practice I teach, comes from the Theravada Buddhist tradition of *vipassanā*, or "insight," meditation. The practice of mindfulness meditation trains you to be present and aware in daily life. When you are being mindful, you are better able to clearly see what is happening in each moment of your life. As a result you gain new insights into your experience, which greatly enhances your ability to tolerate difficult situations and to make wiser decisions.

Mindfulness meditation is now widely taught in health-care institutions as a way to deal with chronic pain and incurable illnesses, and in schools to help children develop concentration skills and impulse control. It is also widely utilized by psychotherapists for helping people work through emotional challenges. Large corporations are starting to provide mindfulness meditation training to employees as a way of improving the work environment and encouraging creativity. Moreover, the U.S. Army is offering mindfulness training to soldiers to help them deal with the stress of overseas deployment.

In mindfulness practice you *practice being an observer of your experience, in the moment, as you are having it.* You begin by noticing how your body responds to whatever is happening. For instance, you develop the habit of noticing if stress is manifesting in your body in the form of raised shoulders, tight jaw or neck muscles, or stirrings in the belly. You start with awareness of the body because it is easy to know and brings you into the present moment. It also grounds your emotions and stops you from getting lost in your thoughts.

Once you have developed the ability to be present with what you are experiencing in your body, you start to pay attention to the other dimensions of your experience. You learn to notice whether what is happening in the body feels pleasant or unpleasant or neutral, and you observe how that feeling affects your thoughts and words. As you become skilled at being aware of bodily sensations, you then start to observe how every emotion and every mind state has a pleasant, unpleasant, or neutral quality, which helps you develop the habit of noticing your mind states and emotions in any given moment. For instance, you may repeatedly experience frustration, irritation, or anxiety by the end of your workday.

Through mindfulness, you begin to notice the early warning signs in your body of unpleasant emotions and mind states arising. And you discover that they are not you but rather the result of impersonal causes and conditions—work overload, a difficult boss or coworker, deadline pressures, etc.—exacerbated by your mind's reaction to the unpleasantness and uncertainty. You then realize that you can choose not to fall into anxiety or irritation and can instead relax your body, interrupt the unskillful mind pattern, and reframe how you view your situation. Even though unpleasant moments still occur, your work life has gained a new ease and clarity. The difference is that you no longer identify with your emotions and mind states or allow them to determine the nature of your experience.

During the mindfulness process, you do not judge, compare, or try to fix your emotions or mind states. Instead you learn to be fully present to whatever you are experiencing, with a calm, nonjudgmental mind and an open heart. Gradually you become aware of when a mind state is being controlled by pleasant or unpleasant feelings and if they are causing thoughts, words, and actions that lead to suffering for you or others. At this stage you spontaneously start to realize that you do not have to be controlled by your mind's reaction to pleasant or unpleasant circumstances and react unskillfully. *By coming to know your thoughts and behavior and the underlying motivations for them, you develop more skillful behavior.* You move from emotional chaos to clarity, from a reactive mind to a responsive mind.

There are many benefits to becoming more present in the moment. Many people report that they gain the ability to be more spontaneous or to know more fully what action or decision is called for in a situation. Others say that their lives are simply richer. Still others describe feeling truly alive for the first time or more authentic than they have felt since their youth. The feeling of authenticity is a marker of achieving maturity as a human being. Feeling real to yourself and being genuine with others are requirements for sustaining a sense of meaning in life.

Mindfulness can also make you a more effective person in the world. Since you are more present, you notice more about what is going on around you and you see more alternatives for achieving your goals. You also have better access to your intuition and can think more clearly.

A few words of warning: It is easy for your ego to get swept away with its newfound sense of empowerment and lead you to act even more unskillfully, thus defeating the purpose of learning mindfulness. Therefore it is essential that you also develop generosity and ethical standards as you gain personal power. Initially there is also a downside to being more mindful in the moment: it becomes much harder for you to fool yourself. You are stuck with seeing when you are not being who you wish to be. The good news is that by repeatedly observing the suffering you cause by not being your authentic self your behavior starts to change. You reach a point where you cannot stand to see yourself act in such a manner one more time!

At first there may seem to be another downside to mindfulness. As you learn to be more present from moment to moment, you become aware of unpleasant moments that you may have suppressed or ignored in the past. Amazingly, after the initial period of learning to be present, you will discover that mindfulness actually makes unpleasant experiences more bearable because it provides distance from, and understanding of, what's difficult. I often tell students that the clarity of mindfulness is a win-win situation. It gives you a fuller, richer experience of what is pleasant and happy-making in your life while also bringing relief to the difficult and unpleasant. Who can afford to pass up such a gain?

Skillful Living through the Power of Intention

In addition to mindfulness, there is a second life skill that is essential to develop if you are going to move from emotional chaos to clarity: intention. *Intention is the capacity to stay in touch with what is of prime importance to you, from moment to moment, in your daily life.* By "what is of prime importance" I mean those *core values* that you wish to live from as you pursue your life's goals and engage with other people throughout the day. Knowing your intentions allows you to remain authentic and have clarity in meetings at work; in interactions with your significant other, family, and friends; and in making decisions about your time, money, and activities.

The fruit of cultivating intention is wisdom. Staying grounded in your intention dramatically shifts how your mind and heart respond to circumstances. It allows your deeper values and your sense of purpose to become the foundation for all your experience. It literally changes *what* you perceive in a situation and how your mind *interprets* what you perceive, and it enhances how you *understand* what you perceive and how you *act* on what you perceive. For instance, let's say a coworker acts in a manner that is unfair to you. You might perceive this as an act of aggression or a personal attack, which you interpret as a reflection of your unworthiness or your helplessness, and it might even prompt you to become aggressive. You might *react* by either collapsing or lashing out at the other person in an unskillful manner that only makes the situation worse. If you are established in your intentions, however, you may still feel the heat of indignation, but you know you have a choice. You can *respond* in a wise manner—choose to be firm or even aggressive, to ignore it, or to deal with it in some other way. Moreover, because you know your intention and what you are about, you can stay genuine in the situation, despite pressure, uncertainty, and vulnerability. Best of all, the episode does not ruin your day. You are in touch with your intention to not let your mind be tugged back and forth by every single pleasant or unpleasant event; you are clear that your inner experience is what matters to you, not the words of someone reacting like a jerk.

You can begin to see that intention requires mindfulness. It is the ability to be awake in the moment that allows you to stay in touch with your core values and pause before lapsing into a reactive mind state. And when you add intention to mindfulness in your daily activity, the result is a sense of genuineness and authenticity. You know who you are, what you are about, and what matters. During conflicts you act from your inner feelings rather than feelings elicited by the behavior of others. You are comfortable with yourself, and this adds to the feeling of being authentic. Can you see why your wisdom would flourish under such circumstances and why your life would have far greater clarity?

One Man's Journey to Skillful Living

The following is the story of one Life Balance client that I hope will give you a sense of how mindfulness and intention can work together to bring about a transformation in your life. For several years I worked with Richard as he struggled to find balance. Bright and hard-working, he was successful and well-known in his field. He came to see me with several complaints: he often felt betrayed by his colleagues, whom he believed did not support or credit his work; and he had never had what he felt was a successful intimate relationship, despite having been married when he was in his twenties. He had always had difficulty being alone, and this often led to unskillful behavior, including drinking too much alcohol.

In our first session it quickly became apparent to me why Richard encountered hostility from his peers—he tended to be self-referencing and pushy. He lacked listening skills and failed to empathize with others unless he was specifically focused on getting them to do what he wanted. Ironically, Richard was quite generous when it came to helping people in financial need or who were experiencing some kind of difficulty. His self-centeredness wasn't rooted in selfishness but rather in his inability to overcome, in ordinary situations, the chaos of his own emotional needs. His inner experience was so chaotic that he was desperate to ensure that his needs were going to be met from moment to moment. From this perspective Richard may seem like a sympathetic figure, but in day-to-day life people were far too overwhelmed by his pushiness to feel sympathy for him.

Although Richard was a romantic guy who genuinely wanted to be in love, remarry, and have children, he interacted with women in an indiscriminately seductive manner, which turned off many of those he was interested in. The same poor listening skills, his habit of self-referencing, and his constant assertiveness made intimacy extremely challenging.

Richard was a perfect example of the cost of emotional chaos, even in a highly functioning person. In both his professional and personal lives, he simply crashed whenever he felt a difficult emotion arise. This would sometimes happen in our sessions. He would obsess about a past mistake and repeat the story of it over and over. He brooded about slights he believed he had received, and he took every disagreement with his peers as a sign of disrespect.

Richard's mind was so complex, and his emotions so conflicted, that he was like a Shakespearean character—a modern-day Hamlet or King Lear. He would dally in ambivalence, be swayed by insincere flattery, be crushed by his defeats. Because he was so smart, it was hard for him to benefit from psychotherapy—he always had a good argument to counter anything he didn't want to hear. He had gone through two therapists and was meeting with a third at the time we worked together. It seemed to me that the therapists were doing a fine job and that Richard simply lacked the tools to take advantage of their techniques—he was anything but mindful and, more often than not, out of touch with his deeper intentions.

Richard and I spent many hours together examining his life skills. I had him write down his goals and then evaluate how important they were to his happiness. I also had him complete some of the same self-assessment evaluations that appear in this book. We role-played various situations in his professional life that had gone badly; he would relive the scene, only now acting in a manner that was more skillful. I had him choose one particular life skill and focus on it for a month and then helped him identify appropriate real-life situations where he could practice that skill. We also examined every aspect of his relationships with women—his motivations and what he thought he was communicating with his words and actions versus how women seemed to interpret them.

Richard began making progress when I had him focus on his emotional crashes and how devastating they were to him. With my encouragement, he learned how to be sufficiently mindful of his life experiences such that he could see how close he came to being dysfunctional whenever he was caught in a difficult emotion. I suggested that when he felt emotional turmoil arising, he ask himself two questions: "Is it possible to respond more skillfully in this moment?" and "Do I have any choice regarding this specific difficult emotion?" I instructed him not to start thinking about his *complex* regarding difficult emotions or to revisit his *story* about how he had developed this problem but instead to focus on the particular difficult emotion he was experiencing—to name it, feel the unpleasantness of it, be aware of how it was affecting his thoughts, and notice what it was prompting him to say or do. Did he have to listen to those promptings? Did he have to identify with those thoughts and feelings? I asked him to reflect on whether getting caught in a difficult emotion isn't like being caught in a rainstorm. Sure you get wet, but you don't think you are the rain! Difficult emotions are indeed just like a storm: they arise due to causes and conditions, they may soak you and make you feel miserable, but they are not *you*. When you see their impersonal nature, you can learn to cope with them skillfully. This is what Richard discovered for himself.

Richard's breakthrough finally came when he realized that he was not a yo-yo on the end of an emotional string! He discovered that what he paid attention to when he was having a difficult emotion, how he perceived and interpreted his thoughts and feelings, and what values he responded from determined what happened next. He realized that his own choices, and not the circumstances, were of foremost importance. Once he understood there were alternatives to being overwhelmed by difficult emotions, he committed to systematically developing more skillful means of responding to his internal conditions and to others. The strength of his mind, which had previously been something of a hindrance, became his ally and he started to change.

It took many months, but Richard gradually began to get a feel for skillful living. First he improved his relationships with his friends. Then he started a romantic relationship that has led to living together and considering marriage. He still struggles with his professional peer group, but he has fewer conflicts and is better at stopping them before they become full-fledged storms. Best of all is how Richard now handles being alone. Once he realized that being alone is a life skill that can be acquired like any other, he began exploring how to be alone in a manner that is peaceful and satisfying. It is still his least favorite situation, but he reports that he no longer gets lost, restless, or dissatisfied when he is alone.

To his great satisfaction, Richard now frequently finds himself teaching others how to live more skillfully in situations that are not work related. The energy he once put into self-referencing is beginning to benefit others. Even in his professional life, Richard's behavior is now more characterized by caring and generosity than by self-centeredness.

The Art and Science of Skillful Living

Learning to live more skillfully through mindfulness and wise intention is part science and part art, part psychology and part spirituality, part common sense and part envisioning. It is a science in that you objectively identify and develop the skills needed and an art because learning how to focus your attention in the various moments of your life involves subjectivity and intuition. It is part psychology because you are developing a much healthier ego and understanding the subtleties of your mind and part spirituality because your core values are based on what you feel gives life meaning. It is common sense because you apply your mindfulness judiciously, not getting lost in overinterpreting what is occurring in the mind, and envisioning because you have to see the possibility that there is a genuine opportunity to change your life.

You, just as you are, not some new-and-improved version of your-self, have the opportunity to function at a new level. But it requires your attention, your willingness to reflect and investigate, and, most of all, it requires that you open your heart to its innate yearning to live more skillfully. Skillfulness in living does not come just because you wish you had it or regret that you don't. It is active engagement that brings about change. Skillful living through mindfulness and intention ultimately allows wisdom to blossom. All your mistakes and unskillful moments become fertilizer for your wisdom to grow. *You cannot practice wisdom, but you can practice being more skillful!*

Starting a Mindfulness Meditation Practice

Mindfulness meditation builds your capacity to be mindful in daily life. As you practice mindfulness meditation, you develop the habit of being present in all moments of your life. Mindfulness meditation practice also creates a safe place for you to get to know your mind.

Start by finding a comfortable place to sit in a chair or on a cushion. Set a kitchen timer or alarm clock to go off in twenty minutes. Over time, you may want to increase the length of your meditation.

Feel your body sitting on the chair or the cushion and remember that your intention is to stay present in your body and mind.

Next notice any places where there is tension in your body. Then relax the muscles in your shoulders and face, and take a few deep breaths.

Now turn your full attention to your breath. It will be your anchor for staying mindful from moment to moment.

You may feel the breath in your abdomen, chest, or nostrils or as a wavelike motion passing through your whole body. Of these sensations choose the one that is easiest for you to notice, and continue to focus your attention on it.

You will quickly discover that your mind wants to wander to other bodily sensations and to many different kinds of thoughts. Each time you discover that your mind has strayed, pause for a moment and just notice where it went. Then gently but firmly place your attention back on your breath. If it helps you to stay present, you can count your breaths, starting with the inhale as ten, the exhale as nine, and so on down to one. If you get lost while you're counting, just start over. Do not judge yourself.

As you're following your breath notice as many of its characteristics as you can. Is this particular breath long or short, fast or slow, heavy or light, shallow or deep? Don't attempt to control your breath, and don't get upset with yourself if you do!

If you discover that your mind is obsessing about planning your day, or recalling a difficult conversation, etc., then repeatedly say to yourself, "planning, planning" or "remembering, remembering." Eventually your mind will be willing to come back to the breath. If a strong emotion comes up, don't be alarmed. Be patient and kind to yourself as you feel the effect the emotion has on your body and your mind.

In a home meditation practice, you "take what you get," so don't expect it to be necessarily calming or restful. Most of the time the mind will not be very concentrated, but know that you are learning to stay present in your experience, no matter what it is.

Chapter 2

Getting to Know the Real You

Your movement from emotional chaos to clarity begins with answering the question, "Who am I?" This doesn't mean your gender, nationality, age, family situation, or ethnic background, and certainly not what you do for a living. Nor is it a question of who you *believe* yourself to be. What I mean is, what matters most to you in those moments when you are not caught up in getting what you want or avoiding what you fear?

Knowing what is essential to you allows you to meet the chaos of life with a clear mind and an open heart. In my experience, being clear about who you are as you respond to life's twists and turns is the only strategy that leads to a sustainable sense of well-being. Being grounded in your authentic self, or what I like to call your *essence*, supports you in making choices and decisions, helps you endure anxiety and stress, and enables you to bear disappointment and difficulty with equanimity.

The great challenge you face, like everyone else, is discovering your essence and then learning how to respond to life in light of this insight and wisdom. The central purpose of this book is to help you achieve this transformation in your life. But first you must learn to discern what is authentic, to separate it from the many false or episodic identities you have undoubtedly acquired in your struggle to find your way in life. For example, a false identity you may have adopted is one that needs to be in control of what happens to you. If things go well, you are pleased with yourself; if they don't, you blame yourself. But it only takes a moment of reflection to realize that this is a false identity.

The hard truth is that life is characterized by continual change and you can't count on it going as you planned. The ever-flowing stream of life delivers small and large misfortunes, all of which are beyond your control, from daily disappointments such as getting caught in traffic and missing an appointment to major life-altering challenges such as the loss of a loved one. Being able to control what happens to you in life is therefore not substantial ground on which to base your identity. The you that is always in control is an illusion. It does not exist. No matter how bright and skilled you are, you will only create turmoil for yourself by clinging to this false identity.

The Myth of Fingerprints

When I teach meditation students about the ways identity is created, I encourage them to think about false identity in terms of what I call *the myth of fingerprints*. On the surface it may seem that we are separate and isolated from one another, but this is only a partial truth that obscures the larger truth that we are all interconnected. Yes, your fingerprints are different from mine and from everyone else's, but we all have fingers, which we use in similar ways. Thus, in knowing what it means to have fingers, we discover that what we have in common is more important than our differences. The dissimilarity of our fingerprints isn't what's important but how we use our fingers. Do we use them for building and creating beauty or do we use them to cause harm?

The same is true of your emotional history. It is uniquely yours, but others also experience the joy, anger, excitement, fear, and love that you feel. Your emotional history doesn't make you a separate species; it is simply one of the endless ways that human beings manifest the emotions they share.

To give another example, if a raindrop falls to earth, seeps into the ground, and then slowly travels through the soil to a creek, and from there flows over many rocks and branches into the sea, it has had an incredible history. But that history doesn't capture the essence of rain. Likewise, your emotional history doesn't capture your essence. Nonetheless, many people live their whole lives without realizing that they are mistaken about who they are.

You too may struggle to understand your authentic self. For instance, you may unconsciously assume that you are the collection of old habits of mind that you've accrued over your lifetime in reaction to difficulty, disappointment, and uncertainty. You may believe you are someone who is anxious because as a child you had to endure a constant stream of criticism from your parents. Or you may see yourself as a failure because you haven't achieved your career goals. But these conditioned mind states are not you—they are merely thoughts and feelings. These thoughts and feelings, as you can observe for yourself, are temporary and ever-changing, and arise episodically. So while they may characterize your experience sometimes, they don't define you. *Your authentic self is defined by the values from which you respond to these mind states.*

One skillful way to begin to understand who you are is to examine those aspects of yourself that you have mistakenly believed were the true you. As the false identities fall away, you develop clarity about what really matters. This clarity comes about as you cease to identify with the chaos of your life and as your heart opens to living life in accord with what matters most to you. The result is that you are no longer confused by the myth of fingerprints.

A word of caution: False identities come about due to conditions that are a genuine part of your experience and have meaning for you. Therefore a critical step in coming into your essence is to address the genuine physical and emotional needs of your false identities.

You Are Not Your Emotions

Who you are not is your current emotional state or the emotional states that you most frequently experience. You may feel overwhelmed by present circumstances or bound by past traumatic events in such a way that one or both seem to define you, and you may not be able to imagine experiencing yourself in any other manner. But painful as your emotions may be, they are not an intractable limitation that prevents you from knowing your authentic self. Your emotions are just reflections of mind states, all of which can be known and released. When you attend to your emotions with mindfulness, you begin to see that they are impermanent and don't belong to you; therefore they do not ultimately define who you are.

Agnes, a student who attended my weekly meditation class, was so identified with her anger that it controlled her life. She was easily upset by real and imagined perceptions of being mistreated, which would cause her to act out in order to defend herself or to seek justice. She knew she was identified with her anger but felt that, because of her childhood history of abuse and neglect, it was just who she was. What a mess this angry person made of Agnes's life! She was fired from a great job at one company, lost an important promotion at another, and drove away a husband and three serious boyfriends. All this turmoil occurred despite the fact that she was bright and friendly and could be quite charming when she wasn't upset. But when she got angry, she was like an alcoholic on a drinking binge. Her anger stayed a long time, it lashed out at everyone around her, and it would intensify when it met resistance.

It took more than three years of daily mindfulness of her anger, and several meditation retreats, before Agnes realized that the anger was no more than a visitor that arrived because of certain causes and under particular conditions—it was not her identity. During this time, I too was the subject of Agnes's anger, but I would only respond to it with compassion and patience. I repeatedly asked her to tell me where in her body she felt the anger. I also directed her to notice if her anger was accompanied by images or an inner voice or a rushlike sensation and if these experiences changed. I would then ask, "What does the angry person need from me right now? What does she need from you? Can you take care of the one who is angry?" Gradually Agnes realized that although the "angry teenager," as she called it, was a part of her experience, it certainly did not constitute an unchanging self, and that when she ceased to identify with it she was much more able to comfort herself and avoid trouble.

You Are Not Your History

Like many people, you may believe that your identity is defined by your history and that you have no other choice than to live out that history, regardless of the chaos it may cause you and others. But this is a fundamental misconception. Your history is simply an accumulation of actions and events that characterizes you at a particular moment in your life; it does not define your essence. Although it is true that you do not have a choice about your history, *you can choose how you respond to your history.* Developing this capacity will lead you to a deeper relationship with your authentic self and a more genuine experience of life. For example, perhaps you had a mother who was emotionally unavailable or a father whom you feared. Your childhood was difficult, but you fortunately found comfort in nature and books. You could choose to create an identity out of your damaged relationships with your parents and go through life struggling with intimacy and never feeling worthy of a relationship. Or you could focus instead on your history of being inspired by nature and reading, and through it cultivate your capacity for relating.

A second aspect of personal history that can create identity confusion is thinking that your history makes you either less worthy and able, or more entitled and qualified, than others. For example, one Life Balance client, a successful Silicon Valley computer engineer, believed he was a fraud simply because he only had an undergraduate degree (and not in computer science). He was convinced that he was less qualified than his colleagues and that sooner or later they would find out and reject him, even though he consistently came up with solutions to problems no one else could solve. Another client, who was a well-known event organizer and promoter, had just the opposite issue. He boasted to me about his plan for sharing credit with his coworkers for a successful project, but in fact he was giving himself more credit than he granted the others, even though his contribution was much smaller. His rationale was that everybody would expect him to receive the majority of the credit because of his reputation in the industry.

Like everyone else's, your history is partly characterized by difficulties and disappointments, as well as unskillful choices and actions. But none of those things are you, nor are you the emotions they elicit—they came about because of causes and conditions that are no longer present. Your pain and suffering are also no more or less substantial, real, or difficult than anyone else's, and from an inner-development perspective, making comparisons with others is false and often self-harming.

You Are Not Your Responsibilities or Your Habits

The commitment to discover what is essential to you often gets lost in the ordinariness of life, where you are beguiled by the false comfort of routine and the tyranny of responsibility. You can fall quite literally into believing your identity is the sum of your duties and habits. For example, if you were forced to take on a major responsibility during your childhood, such as caring for younger siblings, you may have created an identity around being responsible. You may or may not find this identity pleasing, but either way, it's hard for you to *not* take on responsibility. Similarly many women who have careers and are also mothers and homemakers have lives that are so dependent on routine that they become identified with simply fulfilling that routine.

When you mistake your habits and responsibilities for your essence, you close yourself off from feelings of authenticity. Your daily routines and duties aren't the problem; confusion arises when you identify with them rather than fulfilling them from your essence. I often encounter this phenomenon in married couples whose children have left home. They report having no sense of direction, no sense of who they are beyond their responsibility as a mom or dad. Their identities as lovers were displaced long ago by their identities as parents. When I suggest that they imagine themselves being reborn and explore the capacities in them that are ready to be expressed, they often tell me they just want me to help them find something else to be responsible for.

You Are Not Your Public Persona

A key step in the process of understanding who you are is to examine your relationship with your outer identity, or *persona*, meaning the public face or mask with which you meet the world. You must have such an identity to mitigate the friction that arises during the interaction between your inner and outer experiences. Your persona includes an array of qualities, or personality traits, that you present to others as being you. It's how you want others to see you—friendly, intimidating, modest, competent, helpless, nice, honest, powerful, sexy, wounded, and so forth. Think of these personality traits as being like personal software you've developed to serve as your interface with life.

You select, organize, and present a certain package of these characteristics to others as though they constitute an "I" that is solid, consistent, and unchanging. However, your persona is not entirely within your control. It is a combination of those traits you deem appropriate and those you have been strongly conditioned by your environment to have.

Insofar as you are able, you choose the identity you want to reveal to the world from the thousands of thoughts, impulses, and bodily sensations you experience daily. This filtering process never stops; therefore your persona is constantly changing, even though you may not notice it. As an adult you do much of this filtering automatically, although occasionally you may experience a conflict within your persona when an unwanted emotion surfaces and gets acted out in the world. You may have certain traits you wish you didn't; if so, it means they are so strongly conditioned in you that you can't prevent them from being part of the identity you present to the world.

There is nothing inherently wrong with having a persona; it is a social and psychological necessity that develops automatically from childhood through adulthood. Everyone needs a public face in order to function. When students in my classes first begin to realize some of the misconceptions they hold about their outer identity, I gently caution them, "True, you are not your persona, but don't leave home without it!"

It can seem threatening and disorienting to acknowledge to

yourself that you are not your persona. But when you start to have some distance from your outer identity, your sense of authenticity actually increases, because you are not constricted by fear of that persona being exposed or collapsing. If you are in touch with your deepest values, you will know what you want to say and how to act. This is how you empower yourself to live a truly authentic life.

You Are Not Your Ego

Just as you are not your persona, your true identity isn't found in your ego structure—that self-referencing complex of memories, associations, and habitual perceptions that combines with the mind's planning and reflective capacity to serve as the management system for your physical and emotional well-being. It is likely that much of the time you identify with the mental and emotional activity of your ego and feel as though it must be the true you. After all, it definitely wants what it perceives as advantageous and fears or dislikes that which seems to be painful or disadvantageous to you.

One of my Life Balance clients, Leonard, had a dazzling personality. He'd experienced great worldly success, so he was very confident in displaying his ego. Yet he was plagued by emotional chaos in his personal life. During our sessions, whenever he came close to owning up to the truth of this imbalance and making hard decisions to correct it, he would suddenly become Mr. Personality and distract us both with his charm or an entertaining story. It was astounding to witness how skillfully he used his personality as a primary defense against any threat to his ego identification.

It's easy to see how you can become identified with your ego. After all, when you feel confident or uneasy, or when you feel good about yourself or down on yourself, it seems like it has to be *you*, right? But when you begin to observe yourself more closely and dispassionately, you will discover that the seemingly solid ego you thought was you actually is more like a committee composed of characters with different agendas and points of view. Some members of the committee share views and goals, while others hold contradictory positions. The particular ego self that happens to be chairing the committee in a given moment thinks it's you. And you believe it!

Recognizing this committee in your mind can be simultaneously dismaying and liberating: dismaying because you lose the false security of having a fixed mind, and liberating because you now know you don't have to believe your thoughts. Instead you can begin to manage the committee, with its competing interests, as best you're able. And just how do you manage your inner committee? By continually referencing and developing your intentions in the moment and clarifying your goals so they reflect your core values.

You Are Not Your Private Self

Once you begin to understand the truth of your ego and your outer identity, it becomes possible to be more mindful of your inner identity, or what I sometimes refer to as your *private self*. This private self is how you know and experience yourself within the stream of ever-changing thoughts and sensations that register in your mind, and your private self is different from everyone else's. Only you know these subjective mind-body events; therefore it's easy to see why your private self may think it's the true you.

You may recognize your inner identity as clusters of emotions that arise at different times because of stimuli, memories, and associations. Or you may associate your private self with urges or bodily sensations. It may take the form of the ongoing story of your life that you tell yourself and continually update. It is also not unusual for an image to arise that symbolizes part of your inner identity. For example, one of my students desperately wanted to be recognized for her competence and thus identified with the image of Marilyn Monroe, not for her sex appeal, but because of her need to be worshipped.

The ways in which you imagine and organize your private identity are endless, and by definition only you can truly know yourself at this level. I don't mean to imply that your thoughts, emotions, and sensations aren't real. Rather I'm suggesting that your awareness of them does not constitute your essence or reflect your core values. For example, suppose you're driving on the freeway and another driver cuts you off, or you're having a disagreement with a coworker over division of duties, or you're having an argument with your teenage son about cleaning his room. You may well have impulses and thoughts that are destructive in nature. You may feel an urge to ram the car that cut you off, or wish that the difficult coworker would get fired, or want to say something hurtful to your child. Only you feel these impulses and register these thoughts, but do they constitute your authentic self? I suspect not. They are simply mind states and emotions that arise and pass in response to certain causes and conditions.

Does this mean that you should ignore your impulses and thoughts? Not in the least. Instead be mindful that they have arisen and look compassionately at the reasons why they arose, but know that they are not you and you do not have to obey them. This intervention then allows you to see your impulses in the context of your deepest values, and from there you can choose which ones to act on and which ones to simply let pass.

Once when I was teaching mindfulness in a prison, I worked with an inmate who had jumped off the roof of a three-story building and survived with minor injuries. He'd been seeing a prison psychologist for many months to try to determine the underlying cause of this rash, self-destructive action. I took a different approach and asked him to describe his inner experience at the moment he had the urge to jump off the building. Sure enough, the impulse arose one day when his mind was upset. I asked, "What happened next?" He told me, "Once I had the thought, I didn't want to be someone who chickened out." This was a perfectly logical, consistent action based on a value—in this instance, not hesitating to act simply because he might get hurt. I acknowledged him for being committed to "walk his talk" and then suggested, "You know, you are not your thoughts or your impulses. All sorts of them come and go in the mind. They are not to be trusted or obeyed, but they are to be listened to so you can decide which of them you want to honor and then respond to in the manner of your choosing." I went on to say, "Real courage is acknowledging them first, then choosing which ones to act on." This triggered an "aha!" moment. He immediately understood how he had acted from impulse, and he was relieved that he was not "crazy." In the following months, he began to be able to distinguish his impulses as separate from him. This is not an isolated case; time and again in the prison I witnessed inmates mistakenly identifying with impulsive thoughts and then acting on them in order to feel genuine or like a "stand-up" person.

You may say to yourself, "Well, that's how *they* are. I'm not like *that*." But are you really so sure that you don't have a similar pattern of behavior? Is it possible that you do the same thing but in a more socially acceptable form? How many times have you said or done something even though you knew it wasn't wise and didn't really reflect your core values? For example, a number of my "over-forty" students have told me in interviews that they regret the times they had sex in their twenties and thirties when they didn't really want to. At the time they felt an impulse to please (as reported by the women) or to avoid admitting the mixed feelings they were having (as reported by many men). Likewise, I have been shocked by the number of people who have told me that they knew before getting married that it was a mistake, yet they'd impulsively said yes and then felt committed.

Again, I'm not suggesting that your inner experience isn't real.

Nor am I saying that it's not personal. It is your subjective and unique interpretation of life as it unfolds; no one else can ever have a single moment of your experience. But creating a solid identity based on this ever-changing flow of inner experience is a mistake because it is really just a collection of neurochemical reactions in your brain as it processes stimuli in your environment, and therefore it is always changing.

Nevertheless, it is skillful to align with and act from your private self. When you do, you feel more alive and genuine than when you are simply acting out your persona. In fact sharing your private self with another person is what it means to be intimate. Your challenge, though, is to not confuse your private self with your identity, which is where mindfulness can help. Mindfulness empowers you to clearly see that your inner identity, just like your persona, is constantly in flux and not to misinterpret it as being you.

To better understand the distinction between your private self and your authentic self, imagine that your life is like a road trip. Your inner identity is the ideal traveling companion to be seated next to you on this journey because its thoughts and emotions provide depth, texture, and authenticity. But that doesn't mean you should allow it to drive the car. It might, on an impulse, drive straight off a cliff! The more skillful driver to sit behind the wheel is your authentic self, which knows your deepest intentions.

Knowing Who You Are

Now that you've begun to understand who you are not, you can start to discover who you truly are: *a unique combination of capacities and values.* What I mean by "capacities" is this:

- You can experience sensations, thoughts, and emotions.
- You can organize and interpret your experiences.

- You can place them in context of the past, present, and future.
- You can associate any experience you have with other events and people.
- You can visualize and otherwise imagine all sorts of possibilities in relation to any experience you have.
- You have the ability to know if something is pleasant, unpleasant, or neither.
- You have the incredible ability to be continually aware of all these capacities while they are happening.
- You have a wide-ranging emotional capacity, and you have choices in how you respond emotionally to any experience. For instance, you can laugh at what happens, be thrilled by it or afraid of it, feel love because of it, or feel several things at once.
- And with practice you can choose which of these capacities to utilize in any circumstance.
- Likewise, you can remember and plan a response to anything that arises, whether it originates outside you or from within.

We all have these capacities, but how each of us manifests them is unique. To some degree your capacities are determined by your genes, by how you were nurtured as a child, and by life-defining events, but not nearly so much as you may think. Unlike the ability to play the piano or be a great athlete, your capacity for responding skillfully to what happens to you is primarily affected by the immediate attention you pay to it—starting right now. Mindfulness enables you to notice what is happening in any moment and to tolerate it so that you can then investigate it, understand it, and place it in a context that gives meaning to your experience. As you become mindful of your capacities, your mind is less likely to be chaotic and you are less likely to feel powerless in difficult situations. This is because your awareness extends beyond your mind's reactivity.

However great your capacities may be, they are actually only a potential that resides within your mind. They are shaped by your values. To exercise your capacities wisely requires knowing what your values are and living in accord with the motivations that come from those values. This is why, in one sense, your values define the essence of who you are even more than your capacities. Your values help determine what you notice in each moment of the day, which combination of your capacities you will use to respond to any situation, and how you will choose one response over another. They also temper the level of intensity of your response. For instance, if someone is being verbally aggressive toward you at work and what you value is never being humiliated, then you will perceive it as an attack on your ego. But if you value understanding what others are feeling, you might notice how anguished or insecure or driven the attacker is. You'll still defend yourself appropriately, but you will view the situation as being the other person's problem, not yours. It won't ruin your day.

What you value also determines your inner experience of a situation. For example, if someone defeats you in a competition by cheating, you may feel like a victim, or feel foolish for playing by the rules, or you may feel glad that you aren't someone who is so greedy. The third inner experience obviously creates a greater sense of well-being, and if you are going to fight the cheating, it is, ironically, because you are not ensnared in your emotions, the best mental state from which to seek justice.

To live a values-based life, you first have to clarify your values and learn to stay mindful of them in moments of great pressure or emotional intensity. Otherwise your reactive mind state creates its own value system in that moment, which is based on getting what it wants and getting rid of what is unpleasant. As you already know, there is not much wisdom in the reactive mind! Moreover, the reactive mind does not utilize your capacities effectively or efficiently, nor does it act in your best interest. Your reactive mind is too desperate; it just wants relief from the stress it has identified as being you.

Clarifying and staying in touch with your values is hard work and it takes time, but you can start to live this way right now, no matter what your circumstances are, because you have the capacity to do so. When you start to trust your core values, you have created the foundation for an authentic life, and then little effort is required to know what really matters in any situation. It is an amazing transformation. But learning to trust your core values isn't easy and doing so requires developing intention, a life skill that we will explore in-depth in the next chapter.

Discovering Who You Are Not

Understanding who you really are involves overcoming misperceptions about who you are *not*. This transformation doesn't happen simply by thinking about it once. It demands continued reflection and investigation. The following suggestions can help you cease being trapped in a false identity and begin to open up to new possibilities:

- Reflect on what you have read in this chapter and ask yourself what you believe to be true about you and your identity. For example, which type of mistaken identity best describes the way you tend to think? Which type has caused you the most suffering in the past?

- Become a careful observer of your behavior and the mind states underlying that behavior. More than likely, you will start to notice a heretofore hidden separation between the seemingly solid identity that arises in a moment of strong emotion and your awareness that you can observe your behavior and your mind states.

- Begin to notice the difference between the experience you are having and your awareness of the experience. For instance, when you feel hungry, shift your attention to the awareness itself. How is this different from the experience of being hungry?

- Become interested in the nature of your awareness itself. The capacity for awareness has a mirrorlike quality—it reflects what you like or dislike and what you identify with—but it is a neutral observer. Notice that your awareness does not become excited or afraid or identify with what you are feeling or thinking; it simply knows and reflects what is happening in your body and mind. Becoming acquainted with this awareness can provide much-needed comfort and stability when you get caught in emotional chaos.

- Finally, select one or two areas of your life in which you tend to get trapped in a mistaken identity, then try, whenever you sense yourself getting caught in those feelings, to remind yourself that they are an emotional mind state that arises because of certain conditions and will disappear when those conditions change. Making this distinction repeatedly can have the amazing effect of creating a sense of freedom in your life and opening up the opportunity to choose to be who you really are.

Chapter 3

Living an Intentional Life

Since I began leading "Changes and Transitions" workshops, years ago, I've observed that the people who attend them generally fall into two groups: those who are outwardly successful but feel like something's missing from their lives, and those who are faced with a difficult transition that is being imposed on them, such as losing a job or getting a divorce. The people in the first category report feeling as though their lives lack purpose. As one woman described it, "I've come to the end of the rails of motivation that carried me this far in life." The people in the second category feel troubled for various reasons, from career dissatisfaction or burnout to financial challenges or relationship issues. One man said, "I thought I was playing by the rules in my career and my marriage, but the rules no longer seem to work."

Although their reasons for signing up for my workshops are quite different, these two groups of people share a common experience: they've all known the suffering that arises from how fragile, difficult, and uncertain life can be. Their predicament is the same one that each of us inevitably faces: given that suffering is intrinsic to life, how do we handle the ups and downs without getting mired in emotional chaos? The conventional advice is to become more effective at establishing and achieving goals. Yes, goals are important, but to respond effectively to feelings that arise from inner or outer turmoil in your life, you also need to set clear intentions based on your values. Only then does it become possible for you to have clarity from moment to moment in your life.

Buddhist psychology posits that intention manifests as *volition*, the power to make choices, and is a major determining factor in consciousness. In other words, your intentions determine how you interpret and respond to whatever enters into your mind through the sense gates. Moment to moment, they provide a bridge between your values and goals.

There's a metaphor I like to use to illustrate the importance of intentions and how they are related to values and goals. Imagine that you are taking a friend on your favorite hike to the top of a mountain. Your goal is for your friend to see the incredible view from the mountaintop. It's a worthy goal because you value being a good friend, and it's generous of you to want to provide this experience for your friend. However, it's just a goal. Although it provides direction and motivation for your movement, it's not the journey. The actual journey is composed of the moments of your hike—each step you take, the conversation you share with your friend, and the thoughts and feelings you have along the way. Being clear about your intentions and staying connected to them as you make your journey will determine the quality of your experience and your friend's. For instance, if your intention is to be attentive, you will notice if your friend is tiring and will suggest taking a break.

Oftentimes you don't have control over whether you achieve your goals—the view from the mountaintop may be fogged in, you may not make it to the top because you run out of time, or you might trip and sprain an ankle—but living from your intentions is something you do have some control over. So whether or not you achieve the goal of reaching the mountaintop, you still have a fine time because you are being true to your intentions.

Lots of disappointing things can happen to you as you move toward your goals in life, but the sense of meaning and satisfaction that comes from living moment to moment from your intentions is independent of these setbacks. It still hurts when you don't achieve something you really care about, but your happiness isn't contingent upon whether you achieve your goals.

For example, let's say you want your company to take a project in a certain direction, but someone else has a different idea. This person is often rude and domineering during meetings, and you find yourself disliking him. You even get upset in anticipation of being in a meeting with him. You are clear about what your goals are in this situation, but what are your intentions? Do you only want to notice your dislike of the person and how he is thwarting you? What sort of quality of experience does this attitude bring to your day?

Instead of allowing your interaction with this difficult person to spoil your enthusiasm for work, imagine being grounded in the intentions to have an open heart and to not take his aggression personally. Your intentions will alter what you notice and how you respond to him. You may start to see his insecurity, which leads him to try to control everything, or his fear of change, which causes him to be resistant to what you are suggesting. Having these intentions doesn't mean that you won't feel irritated by this difficult person or that you will let him push you around in meetings, but they will prevent you from getting lost in judgment or reactivity, and therefore your interactions with this difficult person won't define your experience. Moreover, your intentions will help you think more clearly and find creative ways to get your suggestions accepted.

The Difference between Intentions and Goals

I do not mean to diminish the importance of goals. Goal making is a valuable skill; it involves envisioning a future outcome in the world, creating a plan for achieving it, applying discipline, and working hard to make it happen. You organize your time and energy based on your goals; they help provide direction for your life. It is the ability to identify suitable goals and to stay true to them that allows you to become a great therapist, an effective health-care worker, a competent lawyer or architect, or a great athlete.

Goal-oriented activity is what enables you to master a foreign language, to learn to play a musical instrument, to create financial security, to be a better communicator, to eat a healthier diet. Goals also add spice to life: they create drama—will you or will you not achieve them? You also benefit from the enthusiasm and energy that goals generate in you. But goals have definite limitations. You may struggle and never achieve a particular goal and therefore find yourself devastated because your sense of well-being was dependent on achieving that goal. I've sometimes seen this in women in their late forties who realize they are not going to give birth to a child, despite it having been their number one goal for two decades. This is an understandably disappointing situation, and for some women it can lead to years of apathy, depression, or bitterness.

With goals, the future is always the focus: Are you going to reach the goal? Will you be happy when you do? What's next? Goals never fulfill you in an ongoing way; they either beget another goal or collapse. Although goals make life exciting, intention provides you with self-respect and peace of mind.

Goals tend to focus on an imagined future and are not necessarily concerned with what is happening to you in the present moment. However, your life is primarily composed of your experience in this moment and then the next, just like hiking up the mountain. You can be very good at achieving goals yet miss the experience of being alive. Only in the present moment can you affect the well-being of others and yourself. All past moments are gone and all future moments are yet to arrive; you are only present here and now. It is your intentions that most determine what you make of this precious moment that will soon vanish. This can be a little hard to grasp, but when you do, it provides the motivation to clarify your intentions.

Setting Intentions Based on Your Values

Living from your intentions is quite different from living from your goals. It is not oriented toward achieving a future outcome. Instead it is a path of practice that is focused on *how* you are *being* in the present moment. Your attention is on the ever-present now in the constantly changing flow of life. You set your intentions by understanding what matters most to you and making a commitment to align your worldly actions with your inner values.

One intention that I choose to live by is to be kind. I've chosen this because of the sense of well-being that kindness bestows in all situations. Even when I have to be firm with someone or go against their wishes, I am very clear that I wish to be as kind as possible. I am indiscriminate in my kindness: I don't allocate it to those I like and withhold it from those I don't, or at least I practice this nondiscrimination as best I'm able. (I confess to sometimes struggling to be kind in regard to some politicians!) Nor is my intention of kindness based on pity or wanting to be liked. What happens when I am not kind in a particular moment? I simply start over, learning from my mistake as much as possible so that I can be more capable of kindness in the next moment. This is the difference between having a goal of becoming a kind person and the intention of being kind in each moment. Do you see the power of intention to enrich your life in this manner?

You are about something; you have a base of meaning that informs all the moments of your life.

Cultivating intention does not mean you abandon goals. You continue to use them, but they exist within a larger context of meaning that offers the possibility of peace beyond the fluctuations caused by pain and pleasure, gain and loss. Goals help you find your place in the world and make you an effective person. But being grounded in intention is what provides integrity and unity in your life.

Through the skillful cultivation of intention, you learn to set wise goals and then to work hard toward achieving them without getting caught in attachment to their outcome. By remembering your intentions, you reconnect with yourself during those emotional storms that cause you to lose touch with yourself. This remembering is a blessing because it provides a sense of meaning in your life that is independent of whether you achieve certain goals or not. Ironically, by being in touch with and acting from your true intentions you become more effective in reaching your goals than when you act from wants and insecurities.

Students often ask me whether values and intentions are the same thing. In my view, values come from understanding what is important to you and are part of your personal philosophy, whereas intentions are the application of your values in daily life. You have an array of values that extends into all aspects of your life. For example, you may value loyalty in friendship, earning an honest living, individual privacy, self-understanding, living a certain lifestyle, etc. You also have a core set of intentions that are based on your values and with which you want to meet every moment of your life, such as integrity, compassion, not causing harm to others, being accountable, and so forth. So if one of your values is self-understanding, it is through your intentions of practicing integrity and accountability that you manifest the wisdom that you gain from self-understanding.

In a particular situation you might have to reflect on your values.

For instance, you may need to consider whether it's ethical for you to take an action or whether you have conflicting values in the situation. Intentions, in contrast, are automatic, and they provide immediate orientation for how to move toward your goals and how to go about clarifying or reconciling your values. As you practice being mindful of your intentions, your ability to act from them blossoms. I say "practice" because it is an ever-renewing process. You don't just set your intentions and then forget about them; you live them every day.

In choosing to live by your intentions, you are not giving up your desire for achievement or a better life, or binding yourself to being morally perfect. But you are committing to living each moment with the intention, for example, of not causing harm with your actions and words. You are connecting to your own sense of kindness and innate dignity. Standing on this ground of intention, you are then able to participate as you choose in life's contests, until you outgrow them.

Naturally, sometimes things go well for you and other times they do not, but you do not live and die by these endless fluctuations or outcomes. Your happiness comes from the strength of your internal experience of intention. You become one of those fortunate people who know who they are and are independent of our culture's obsession with winning. You still feel sadness, loss, lust, and fear, but you have a means of directly relating to all of those difficult emotions, and therefore you are not a victim, nor are your happiness and peace of mind dependent on how things are right now.

Intention as a Purification Process

In cultivating intention, one issue that trips up many people is mixed motives. During individual interviews, my students will sometimes confess their anguish at discovering how mixed their motives were in past situations involving a friend or family member. They feel as though they're not a good person and aren't trustworthy. Sometimes my response is to paraphrase the old blues refrain, "If it wasn't for bad luck, I wouldn't have no luck at all." It is the same with motives: if you don't, in most situations, go with your mixed motives, you won't have any motivation at all. You will simply be stuck. Forget judging yourself for having mixed motives and just work with the arising moment. The less judgmental you are about your mixed motives, the more clearly you will see how those unwholesome motives cause suffering. This insight releases the unwholesome motives and makes room for wholesome ones to evolve.

Whether an action is wholesome or unwholesome is determined by the intention that originated it. An apt analogy for this fundamental truth is a knife in the hands of a surgeon and an assailant. Either one might use the knife to cut you, but one has the intention to help you heal, while the other has the intention to harm you. You might die from the actions of either; intention is the factor that differentiates them. From this perspective alone, you are well served by cultivating right intention.

Every action has both a cause and a consequence. When a difficult moment arises in your life, something obviously caused it, but there's nothing you can do about that cause now. However, the way in which you respond to the arising difficulty will have consequences that can be favorable or unfavorable, depending primarily on the clarity of your intentions. Therefore practicing right intention is crucial to living skillfully.

Whatever is manifesting in your life right now is affected by how you receive it, and how you receive it is largely determined by your intentions in this moment. Imagine that you will have a difficult interaction later today. If you aren't mindful of your intentions, you might respond to the situation with a harmful physical action— maybe because you get caught in fear, panic, greed, or ill will. But with awareness of your intentions, you will refrain from responding physically. Instead you might only say something unskillful, causing less harm. And if you have a habit of speaking harshly, with mindfulness of your intentions you might have a negative thought but refrain from uttering words you would later regret. When you're grounded in your intentions, you are never helpless in how you react to any event in your life.

Reevaluating Your Values, Intentions, and Goals

In Buddhist psychology, your path to well-being begins with understanding the values you want to live by (your intentions) and the direction you want your life to go in (your goals). Out of your understanding you develop a core set of intentions to live by no matter what goals you are pursuing or how the circumstances of your life unfold. Apply the following reflections to all aspects of your life, including your primary relationship, family, friends, inner life, and work.

1. Are you clear about what your values are? Have you actually been living from them? And are they the values you want to continue living from?

2. Are you clear about what your intentions are? As you go about your daily life are they shaping how you act and speak? And are these the intentions with which you want to continue to meet each moment of your life?

3. Are you clear about what your goals are? Do your current goals reflect your values? As you work toward your goals do you stay true to your intentions? If your goals don't reflect your values or you're not able to follow your intentions, is it time for you to create new goals?

Chapter 4

Starting Over

As you start to increase your capacity for living from your intentions, you naturally become more aware of all those moments when you are not living from your intentions. Seeing how your untrained mind (and sometimes your cowardly heart) can separate you from your intentions can be discouraging. But if you cultivate the practice of *starting over* whenever you realize you've lost your way, you develop the capacity to be both true to your inner self and comfortable in the world.

I am not exaggerating this increase in your capacity. As you learn to stay connected to your intentions while you pursue both your daily and long-term goals, a satisfying feeling of being present in your life begins to emerge. One Life Balance client described this sensation as feeling as though, for the first time ever, he was showing up for his own life. Your life doesn't suddenly become easy, but you start to have a new relationship with life that's based on being mindful of your intentions. Gradually you reach the point where you know that it is possible to live an intentional life, and you no longer doubt your capacity to stay connected to what is of essence to you.

Of course it's frustrating when you clearly know the benefits of acting from your intentions yet sometimes become lost in fear or desire, or caught up in an emotional storyline. At such times it's easy to conclude that being mindful of your deepest intentions is beyond your capacity. While understandable, this reaction reflects a misunderstanding about intentions that makes the practice more difficult and complicated than it really is. Living your intentions is simply about coming home to yourself in each moment. To develop this capacity you must be willing to start over again and again, to patiently and persistently reconnect to the practice of meeting each moment from your intentions, no matter how long or why you have been lost to yourself.

How Your Intentions Can Be Derailed

I first heard the phrase "just start over" used to describe a mindfulness practice some thirty years ago, by the Buddhist meditation teacher and author Sharon Salzberg. During a mindfulness meditation retreat she led at the Insight Meditation Society in Barre, Massachusetts, Sharon told us about her own struggle with learning to meditate—how she would become lost, distracted, and discouraged and would constantly second-guess herself and her teachers. Gradually she learned to pay no attention to the mental and emotional chatter and to simply start over by meditating on her breath as she had been instructed. "Just start over" became her mantra, and one she now teaches to her students.

Each time Sharon repeated this phrase during the retreat, I was deeply inspired. I realized that she was pointing to a radical attitudinal shift in which you cease to be reactive when you are knocked off your intended path. Instead, when you discover that you have lost your focus, you just begin again without getting caught up in emotional stories about why you can't achieve your aim or judgments about how unworthy you are or why the change you seek is impossible. With Sharon as my inspiration, I set about developing "just start over" into a daily life practice.

As you know if you've ever tried to meditate, the mind is constantly being pulled away from its object of concentration by bodily sensations and mental activity, causing you to lose awareness of the present moment. In this same way, when strong feelings arise during your daily life, you get swept up in the story they create. You lose awareness of the intentions that enable you to respond skillfully to events and to maintain your center in the face of difficulty. For instance, let's say you are often anxious at work or prone to argue with your significant other, and your intention is to stop being this way. Usually, after you resolve to change your behavior, something happens that throws you off track, and the undesired behavior returns in full force. Once again you are completely lost in your anxiety at work or are fighting with your beloved. All the old stories flood your mind, along with self-judgment, discouragement, and frustration. You start to believe that you cannot change.

There are many reasons why you may lose touch with your intentions. Often the problem is that you don't know how to be resolute without also being rigid in your expectations. Or maybe you haven't learned how to sail the waves of the ocean of your mind and successfully navigate those emotionally charged parts of yourself that cause inner storms in your daily life. You may have the mistaken notion that you must know why you get distracted and caught at times and must fix it before you can act in a more self-empowering manner. Starting-over practice takes a different approach. It switches your focus away from dwelling on the characteristics that limit you and redirects it toward recognizing the strengths from which you can realize your potential.

This shift in focus is attitudinal: you simply do what you care about as well as you can. This is a humble attitude, but it is exactly what's needed for you to sustain your intentions. In so doing, you free yourself from your judging mind, which thinks it can control results. You also relieve yourself of the grandiose expectation that you can do more than in fact you can do in the present moment. You become a more effective person by simply learning to use your time and energy to do what you can do *right now*. An intentional life consists of a continuous as possible flow of such moments of being present right now. But this won't mean every moment—to achieve that you would need to be a Buddha.

The Buddha emphasized the need to focus on the present moment and respond appropriately according to one's values, and he rejected speculation for its own sake. In teaching this lesson, the Buddha used the analogy of a man who has been shot with an arrow. If before extracting the arrow and tending to his wound, the man insists on knowing the name, family, and village of the archer, as well as what the arrow is made of, how effective will he be in dealing with his wound? He might die before his questions are answered! What needs immediate attention is the situation created by the arrow. Starting-over practice is like this: you attend as best you can to the immediate situation in a way that is as close as you can come to your intentions. You don't get caught in making up a story about why you forgot your intentions or in speculating about how many times you may get lost in the future.

Starting Over Yields New Flexibility in Your Life

You may assume that you are already skilled at starting over. But although you may conceptually understand starting over (and no doubt you have done so thousands of times in your life), that doesn't mean you've brought mindfulness and intention to it such that it has become a practice. Unless you have a strong practice of starting over, you will be thrown off balance by life's inevitable rough waters as you work to transform yourself.

If you believe that you are already skilled in starting over, try keeping the mind on your breath for thirty minutes. Observe whether you are able to simply come back to it without any comment or other distraction and really give it your full attention, not just once or twice, but repeatedly for the entire thirty minutes. Almost no one can do this without training, and what this exercise reveals is that your mind is stubbornly independent and that your ego lacks a "just start over" attitude.

Initially I taught starting over as a daily life practice only on a one-on-one basis, to students attending meditation retreats. A silent retreat, with its long hours of sitting in meditation, is the ideal situation for practicing starting over and for realizing that the mind can be retrained. After seeing how powerful a tool it was for helping people transform, I began recommending the practice to students in my weekly meditation class. For one forty-five-year-old man with a chronic health problem that would manifest suddenly and unexpectedly, starting-over practice involved transforming the way he responded to the conditions of his life each day. After years of being rendered helpless by his disease and losing his zest for life, he discovered that he could have a rich inner and outer life by focusing on what was available to him *right now*, despite the difficulty of his circumstances. He found that his intention to appreciate life and to participate as fully as possible centered and calmed him. He reported experiencing more and more moments in which he felt alive.

Another student, a bright forty-two-year-old woman whose career had been derailed because of a series of traumatic emotional challenges and who felt shut off from peers at work, learned how to regroup several times each day by acknowledging her feelings of alienation and inadequacy and simply starting over in that moment. She found that if she spent any time indulging in the stories generated by her feelings, they only got worse. I advised her to make immediate contact with others in the office whenever she felt alienated and to do it as a practice, without caring how she felt while doing it. And I suggested that when she started feeling incompetent, she select some small task and do it at once. Within a year of practicing starting over, she reported that although she still experienced feelings of alienation and inadequacy, they no longer controlled her life.

Similarly, a twenty-nine-year-old woman who had a history of anorexia in her youth and still suffered from feeling that she was too "large" learned that she could stop a chain of destructive eating behavior by noticing when certain feelings of anxiety and unspecified dread arose. Through the starting-over practice, she came to realize that whenever those feelings arose it meant she had been "shot by the arrow" and that it was time to practice mindfulness and compassion toward herself and to quit all self-criticism. She learned that if she would just start over by moving her attention to any of a series of tasks that she found stimulating, she was far less likely to be dominated by the negative feelings or to spiral out of control. Her situation was particularly difficult because she was initially convinced she could never change unless she understood why she was the way she was. It was only because she lacked alternatives that she finally responded to my suggestion that she make starting over a practice. Most of the people in these examples have worked with therapists, which I've encouraged, but they report that it is the starting-over practice that they rely on to change their behavior.

Practice, Practice, Practice

So just how do you practice starting over? Think of it as shifting your attention away from your usual reactions—criticizing, judging, complaining, and lamenting—all the mental activity that usually arises when you discover that you have lost your intention due to a strong emotion. Don't deny your thoughts and feelings, and don't try to make them go away. Instead acknowledge them without making any judgments about them. Deliberately cultivate an appreciation for how difficult this moment is and have compassion for yourself. Then follow the acknowledgment with what I call the "and" practice, in which you say to yourself, "Yes, I just got lost, *and* now I'll just start over." For example, "I feel alienated and think my peers don't like me, *and* I am going to go speak to that guy over there whom I think might be friendly." Or, "My body feels weak and sickly right now, *and* I am going to focus on making my child some tea, which at this moment is all I have sufficient energy to do." You always acknowledge your thoughts and feelings, but then you move on to the "and" practice to return to the present moment.

In doing this you don't forget your goals, but your focus is on meeting the present moment in a manner as close as possible to the way you aspire to being in such moments. Naturally, you periodically check in with yourself to see if the way you are going about seeking change or attaining your goal is working. If it is not, you try something different. Likewise, you occasionally ask yourself whether you still care about a particular goal and whether your goal or your intentions have changed in some way. But mostly you just persevere in being who you wish to be. You develop the strength to start over because you're committed to moving toward your goal, to living from your intentions. This is why I call it an attitudinal shift. Your goals matter because they give direction to your life, but your actual life happens in the endless stream of moments that occur between now and when, if ever, you reach your goal. Because your focus is on the journey and not the goal, you find the willpower and the inspiration to start over. When you're able to relate to life just as it is, rather than insisting that it be the way you would have it, you stand a far better chance of affecting how things are, because you're not caught in emotional chaos.

If you think about it, the practice of starting over is obviously a more effective way to achieve your goal than constantly fixating on it. Most of us are simply not very good at delivering results. For instance, if you are trying to lose weight, curb your temper, or cease being a workaholic, you probably know what to do to stop the undesirable behavior, but you don't do it. Discouragement with recent attempts mingles with disappointments from your past and imaginings about how bad the future will be. Together, these drain your energy and cause you to fail and to expect to fail. When you embrace starting over as a practice, you focus instead on what you are doing right now and what you need to do or are failing to do. Thus if you discover you are overeating in this moment, you simply stop eating. If you have agreed to take on yet another work project, you reverse yourself as soon as it dawns on you that it is too much. If you sense that you're losing your temper, you just stop. No drama; you just get right back on your path and start over.

Patience and Persistence: Prerequisites to Starting Over

Starting over sounds really easy, doesn't it? But it's ever so hard to do and requires that you develop two capacities: patience and persistence. Patience allows you to tolerate the times you fail to remember your intentions and the times you then forget to start over. Persistence brings into play the essential energy for directing your attention back to what needs to be done right now. Remember this rule: *energy follows attention*. Deliberately placing attention on patience gives you the energy to cultivate patience; steady attention on being persistent will yield the energy to nurture new habits of mind. Having a compassionate attitude toward yourself, an attitude that acknowledges how hard it is to stay the course and live according to what really matters, supports both of these qualities of mind.

Within the context of starting over, patience is the capacity of energetic endurance—the ability to abide with things being the way they are. Patience is willingness to bear failure, disappointment, defeat, unpleasantness, and confusion without collapsing. When you fail to live up to your intentions, patience allows you to forgive yourself, to not fixate on your mistake, and to just start over. Developing patience naturally leads to having a less reactive mind and to being patient with others.

In contrast, persistence is the capacity of energetic resolve—the determination to hold steady to your intentions. It manifests as knowing where you are going and being willing to act right now. Persistence *is* starting over. Whereas patience is tolerant and receptive to what is, persistence is movement toward actualizing your intention. Persistence gives purpose to patience. If you lack persistence, then what seems like patience is just dillydallying. Patience without persistence never goes anywhere; you're stuck. Without persistence, you never apply the effort needed to develop the capacity for starting over. Persistence without patience creates imbalance because it drains your energy and can lead to frustration or pushiness, which can be intimidating or alienating to others and can lead to giving up or burning yourself out. A balance of patience and persistence yields sustainability, which brings about long-term change.

Martin Luther King Jr. was someone who fully understood the value of patience and persistence. Without it he would not have been able to overcome the status quo and bring about major social change in the nonviolent manner he did. Like King, you too must be persistent, because it is the cumulative effect of your persistence that builds inner awareness, which yields the pressure to change.

Whether you want to increase your effectiveness at work,

improve the quality of your interactions with friends or your spouse, or even modify your diet, you have to be patient with yourself while you try various strategies to bring about change. It takes time to figure out what will help you make changes; therefore you must persist in your effort or you will neither discover what works nor apply it consistently enough for change to occur. In general, whenever you attempt something new, it takes a while to learn how to be effective with it.

Change Is Genuinely Possible

Living proof of the effectiveness of the practice of starting over is Taryn, a student in the Sunday evening meditation class I teach. Taryn was a successful midlevel manager in a fast-growing company. Although she makes a positive first impression, she has a long history of personal angst, and her career had been stalled for some time. When Taryn first started attending class, six years ago, she was close to losing her ability to function effectively in her high-pressure job. She had difficulty with trust in friendships, she got into adversarial relationships at work with both peers and bosses, and her romantic life had been one disaster after another. A therapist might say that a hypercritical, affection-withholding, competitive mother and a nice but weak and nonprotective father were the source of Taryn's problems. In fact three different therapists had told her just that. But despite knowing why she had trust and communication issues, Taryn continued to suffer, which is what brought her to meditation.

For Taryn, who reported one defeat after another, developing compassion for herself was essential before she could begin to develop the practice of starting over. When she got into yet another disagreement at work, or had a lousy date, or couldn't speak openly with a friend, she would get so angry with herself that she would shut down.

Those around her would be bewildered by her sudden, complete withdrawals.

By doing compassion meditation she learned to tolerate her own feelings so that she could stay present with them, and then she was able to start redirecting her attention to just starting over. Because she was disciplined and highly motivated, she became, once she got a feel for it, quite effective at starting over. She even learned to laugh at herself when she sees one of what she calls her "hindrance attacks" coming on. In Buddhism, the difficult mental states of greed, aversion, sloth and torpor, restlessness and worry, and doubt are referred to as *hindrances*. If you fail to be mindful of a hindrance, then you can be caught by it; if you recognize it, then you have options—you can just start over.

One recent evening Taryn came up to me after class to discuss whether she should take on a new opportunity at work. Twice she had been passed over for a senior management position, so this represented a chance, at last, to demonstrate her capabilities. It was also the perfect setup for all of Taryn's patterns of self-destruction to be activated because it would mean taking on a major, long-term project that involves creating new business practices across divisions in her company. A few years ago I would have been reluctant to encourage Taryn to accept the promotion because she would most likely have failed. But she has since developed a new base of personal power that has changed who she is in relationship to others at work and in her personal life. She now knows how to "just start over" whenever something goes wrong or when she is worried that something might go wrong. I had great confidence that she had the skills to get through the inevitable "bumps" of this new job.

In helping Taryn decide whether to take the promotion, I asked her if she wanted it as an end in itself. "What do you mean?" she asked. "How could I not? It is such an opportunity!" I gently told her that she must be careful to avoid falling into the trap of making the decision on the assumption of a future that may or may not come to fruition. "Does this job seem as though it would be fulfilling even if it leads nowhere?" I asked. She paused, and then her face lit up. "Yes, it is the perfect chance for me to express myself," she said. "This job reflects my values." She paused again. "You don't need to tell me: I know it will be a challenge. And I know I will get off course, a lot, but now I know how to start over," she said with a laugh. She had her answer. As it turns out, Taryn has been able to rise to the challenge and do a terrific job, and she has certainly had to start over again and again. Slowly but surely, Taryn has learned to move beyond her limitations and to live out her potential as best she can.

What I told Taryn applies as much to you. If you wish to change some part of your life and are having a difficult time doing so, take these values to heart: don't ever let anyone tell you that you cannot change; vigorously fight those inner impulses to distract yourself when difficulty arises; and don't allow that critical voice in your own head, the one that constantly tries to tell you there is no possibility of improvement, to rule your life.

And when you discover that you have lost track of your intentions, just start over.

Just Start Over

Starting over is a powerful practice, but don't be surprised if you don't have the ability to commit to it initially. Fortunately there are three simple things you can do to build this capacity in a relatively short period of time.

First, establish the motivation to practice starting over by observing what happens when you waste time feeling discouraged, escaping, or indulging your restless mind. In the week ahead, notice how many times you get knocked off balance when something goes wrong at work or in your personal relationships. Don't judge yourself for getting lost. Just be mindful that this is what is happening to you. If anything, be compassionate with yourself. After all, getting caught in your reactive mind is painful. Once you're able to acknowledge how much emotional energy and time you waste, you will start to realize that the starting-over practice matters and that it is worth the effort it requires. You will have the aspiration, motivation, and conviction to persevere. As F. Scott Fitzgerald once wrote, "Vitality shows in not only the ability to persist but the ability to start over."

Second, select a couple of aspects of your daily life that you want to change and begin to practice starting over. Maybe you'll choose a person you find difficult to interact with, or a particular task at work, or perhaps some behavior related to diet or speech. When you discover that you have gotten lost, say to yourself, "Yes, I just got lost, *and* now I'll just start over." "And" practice empowers you to remember your intentions and goals, and it helps you move through negative feelings and return to the present moment. Try practicing this way for three months, in these two areas, while maintaining mindfulness of all the times you don't start over in the other areas of your life. You will start to notice a difference. Seeing this for yourself creates more faith and, therefore, still more motivation. Then, when you feel ready, add yet another aspect of your life to your starting-over practice. Be prepared for disappointments and for forgetting your commitment; after all, you are teaching your mind a completely new automatic response.

Finally, let meditation be your laboratory for training your mind to think and respond in this new way. Meditation is a safe environment for developing the capacity for starting over because it's just you; nobody knows when you're starting over. Plus it builds your ability to maintain concentration and focus, so you are less likely to be thrown off center in daily life. It also cultivates equanimity and calmness, qualities that help you simply return to your intention whenever you need to start over. Practicing starting over in meditation is very simple: No matter how many times your mind wanders, simply go back to noticing your breath (or whatever you choose for your object of concentration), without making any judgments. Only be interested in how well you're staying with your breath and how well you start over.

Chapter 5

Letting Go of Expectations

Much of the emotional chaos in life is created by unacknowledged or unmet expectations. Like most people, you are probably unaware that your mind is filled with expectations and that they largely determine which life events you pay attention to and how you interpret them. Most of the time you are unconscious of your expectations, yet they control much of what you do and pose an obstacle to living from your intentions.

It's also unlikely that you know how your expectations evolved. The root of any expectation is a desire, which became a goal that then transmuted into an assumption that it is the way your life is supposed to be. You have a set of expectations that have been conditioned by your childhood experiences, peer group pressures, and societal values, and that you have internalized to the extent that you now see them as who you are. For instance, you may have always been sought after by the opposite sex, so you have the expectation that you're an object of attraction. Or maybe you were the smartest kid in school and everyone told you what a great success you were going to be; therefore you have internalized this as an expectation.

Unfortunately, when they're left unnoticed, expectations can become all-powerful and cause you to have negative views about yourself and others that can manifest as confusion, disappointment, fear, defeat, dissatisfaction, or defensiveness. They may plague your daily life, causing you to be irritable, disillusioned, and anxious. And they can lead you to speak or act unskillfully and to make poor decisions. I call this effect *the tyranny of expectations*, since they can literally kill your joy and distort your view of life.

A good example of how destructive your hidden expectations can be is Sarah, who attends my weekly *vipassanā* meditation class. We spend a lot of class time trying to understand how we create our own emotional chaos and suffering by getting caught in an endless cycle of desire and attachment. One evening Sarah came up to me after class to share some good news: "Well, I landed that new job I applied for, and my husband and I got through the crisis I told you about." Despite the good news, her voice was surprisingly rueful, as if she were reporting that life was worse than before. I felt a wave of happiness for her, but before I could say so, she went on to complain about the new job and her relationship. What had recently seemed to be the key to her happiness—if she could only get the job and stop quarreling with her spouse, life would be great—was now a source of dissatisfaction. Our discussion revealed that she repeatedly experienced being disappointed whenever she actually got what she sought. In response, she would create new expectations, and the cycle would repeat itself. Sarah was certainly exhibiting how suffering arises out of hidden expectations.

You too may be suffering from the myriad ways in which expectations can undermine your life. Like Sarah, you may not realize that what you notice in life and how you interpret what happens to you are based on your assumptions about how you and the rest of life are "supposed" to behave. You may have developed a rigid view of how your life is supposed to unfold or made a list of what will bring you happiness or satisfaction. Thus far, that view or that list may not have proven to be realistic, or even if some of your expectations have been met, they may not have brought much joy to your life. But despite such signals, you continue to adhere to old expectations. Why? Because you have yet to become fully aware of the truth that your expectations are steering your life. I have witnessed this phenomenon time and time again, especially among my Life Balance clients who, despite being successful at accomplishing goals, are often bewildered as to why they are not happier. I caution such high accomplishers to beware: *many of your expectations are old goals that have become fossilized.* When goals harden into expectations, you lose all pleasure or satisfaction in your accomplishments, and your life will seem flat. Expectations can also rob you of feeling gratitude for your good fortune. This makes sense: why would you be thrilled or grateful if every good thing that happens to you is somehow expected?

Big Expectations Equal Big Delusions

Expectations show up in many forms—from what we expect of ourselves to what others expect of us and we expect of them. You may have high, low, or even negative expectations about what's possible in your life. Just as an unrealistic high expectation can bring unnecessary disappointment, a low one can bring about underperformance or failure to see the opportunity in a situation. Likewise, a negative expectation can lead to poor judgment or unwillingness to try something new, even though a considered appraisal would result in a different decision. If you are living parts of your life according to negative expectations, you never give yourself a chance. You expect to fail in relationships, or to not attract anyone, or to not be a leader. You may believe no one is trustworthy and seek constantly to confirm that this is so.

Many large and thousands of small expectations arise in your life every day. You may be aware of some of your most dominant expectations but only notice them dimly or some of the time. Or there may have been times when you felt acute disappointment and then realized that you had a big expectation but failed to notice it. Your large expectations reflect the striving every human experiences, but yours have their own unique expression. You may expect to reach a level of economic success or to be happily married and assume because of your background, education, and mental ability that these are your due. Or you may expect to be popular or a "fast-track" person because you were in school, or a leader because you were in the past. You may assume that you will have children and that your children will be a certain way. You may have expectations about how your spouse or family members or coworkers are supposed to treat you. These scenarios might unfold as you expect, but maybe they won't, or maybe they'll only partially materialize. You may find that fulfilling your expectations is much harder than you presumed or even that your expectations don't really reflect what you care about anymore.

As you become mindful of these large expectations, you start to see how they dominate your life choices and color your perception. You begin to see that many of them are just *views and opinions* that you created or others created for you. You see that to a large degree life happens independent of, and often contrary to, your expectations. At first this may seem dismaying, but as you develop more and more awareness, you eventually start to realize that carrying around this jumble of expectations in your head is a burden and that it gets in the way of being present in, and responding to, the life you have.

As you learn to free yourself from these larger expectations, you will start to notice the smaller ones and not allow them to define your experience either. You have countless small expectations, which may be causing you many hours of dissatisfaction, impatience, and tension every day. You may be enslaved by an expectation that you are someone who is always in a good mood, or who's always responsible, or who never gets sick, or never gets impatient with others, and feel terrible or become defensive when you fail to meet these expectations.

Just think of the amount of suffering these unrecognized expectations cause you and others!

Free Yourself from Expectations

The good news is that you don't have to continue to suffer from the tyranny of expectations. It is one of the most troublesome areas of life, yet it is also changeable. Even a little effort makes a huge difference. But first you must penetrate the nature of expectations, observe how they manifest themselves in your life, and be able to find another way of approaching the future.

Expectations are almost always the result of what in Buddhism is called *wanting mind*. This wanting mind is driven by desire, aversion, and anxiety; it creates an illusion of solidity and control in a world that is constantly changing and unfolds independently of how we believe it should. Knowing this, how do you proceed? How can you free yourself from expectations? Using mindfulness, you always start with what is true in the present moment. You use discernment to know what is true, but you do not fall into judgment, which is yet another form of expectation and one of the most tyrannical.

Knowing the Difference between Expectations and Possibilities

A critical step in gaining clarity about expectations is learning to distinguish between them and possibilities. Expectations assume a certain result and are future oriented. They actually narrow your options, retard your imagination, and blind you to possibilities. They create pressure in your life and hold your present sense of well-being hostage to a future that may or may not happen. Expectations create rigidity in your life and cause you to react impulsively to any perceived threat to the future you believe you deserve.

When you are controlled by your expectations, you are living a contingent life and, therefore, aren't free in the present moment. You cannot be happy simply watching a dazzling sunset or experiencing a moment of warmth between you and another; instead you interpret every experience in the context of an expected future. Expectations cause you to feel *entitled* to experiencing beautiful sunsets and intimacy. You believe that's who you are and what, because of your efforts and innate qualities, you deserve.

In contrast to expectations, possibilities are based in the present moment, where you're alive to the mystery of life. Being open to exploring possibilities stimulates the mind, makes life interesting, and provides you with the energy and motivation to live as fully as you can in the present moment, in light of your intentions. You don't assume that the future you desire will come to pass, because the future is unknown. Being open to possibilities also acknowledges that what you think you want may change with time, or that there may be a different future you haven't thought of that will bring you more happiness, or that the future may turn bleak, or that you may die before the future can unfold. Real joy is found in what is available to you right now.

Living a life that is open to possibilities is like a request, rather than a demand. Your well-being is not contingent on the future. Your mind is open and inspired in this moment. You therefore have greater access to imagination and intuition. Your mind is clear and less reactive, and you make better decisions. You respond rather than react to life as it unfolds.

This ability to respond to change rather than react to it is the primary distinction I have observed between people who feel free and those who are caught in emotional chaos. You may often find yourself reacting to the behavior of others or to changes in your circumstances and never realize it is because you were expecting others or your life to be a certain way. When you react this way, you are opting not for the mind of possibility, but for the mind of expectation, and you are left feeling disappointed, hurt, lost, angry, or defeated.

Expect to Stumble

In freeing yourself from expectations, you are likely to encounter a number of challenges. You may be one of those individuals who believe they don't have expectations. But in my experience, people who make such claims have a strong case of denial, which is usually rooted in past disappointments and fear of failing to have expectations met. They often have hidden expectations accompanied by a feeling that "If I can't have what I want, I don't want anything." When you deny having expectations, you are giving up on yourself, and it is impossible for you to be authentic with others. You limit the possibility of actively participating in the truth of your life in every moment and cut yourself off from the power of the love of those close to you. Claiming to be beyond having expectations may sound egoless, but if you look closely, you will see that what you are really doing is denying yourself access to possibilities.

Many people struggle to overcome negative expectations. Beth, who also attends the weekly meditation class I lead, complained for a couple of years about how inadequate her meditation practice was and how she never made any progress. She bemoaned her inability to concentrate and criticized herself for repeatedly getting lost in thoughts. Her self-appraisal was very sincere, and her face reflected tremendous pain when she spoke. She was disheartened but felt she was being honest with herself.

I, on the other hand, thought her practice was going great. I repeatedly told Beth this and pointed out to her that she was suffering from having expectations about what a good meditation practice should look and feel like. She was never relieved by my words, but to her credit she continued to meditate. Then, just as she was making a major transition in her life, retiring from her job and starting to travel as she had waited decades to do, one of her daughters became ill with a life-threatening disease. This required Beth to completely abandon her own plans and move to another city to care for her daughter full time. I did not see her for several months; then one day she returned to meditation class, her face aglow. "My practice saved me!" she exclaimed. "I was calm and mindful. I did not fall into resentment or anger." She paused and then continued, "I was just there for my daughter. I was compassionate toward her and myself. I want you to let everyone in the class know." The difficulties of her life had revealed the true strength of her practice, in contrast to her expectations about what a strong practice felt like.

Like Beth, you too may have negative expectations in some aspect of your life that may not only be causing you unnecessary pain but may also be preventing you from growing or responding to an opportunity. This is why letting loose of expectations and living from intentions is so important. When Beth's plans were derailed and an expectation of a happy, exciting time was transformed into the reality of a time defined by concern and stress, she was able to respond with equanimity. Her practice served her, and she was able to do exactly what life called for in the moment. She was able to let go of her goal of enjoying a life of adventure. She thought life was going one way, but it went another. That was all there was to it. Do you see how this can apply to your own life? It is not that you must avoid making plans or moving toward goals; it is that you don't become defined by those expectations or attached to the outcome.

Can you feel the freedom that exists in being able to respond rather than react when life goes other than how you expected? It doesn't mean that you won't unconsciously create expectations over and over again—no one is imagining you to be perfect (which in itself is just another expectation!). You will most likely continue to fall into expectations. However, by practicing being mindful of expectations and being compassionate with yourself whenever you discover you are caught in expectations, you acquire the skill to let go of them. You see them for the suffering they represent, and you just start over in that moment, as best you're able.

Exploring the Tyranny of Your Expectations

1. Over the next few days, track how many times an expectation arises, including any hidden assumptions. Each time you spot an expectation, ask yourself, "Is this helpful or not?"

2. Begin to notice the number of times each day that you feel the pressure of someone else's expectations of you. How does it feel when you encounter these expectations? What does your mind do with them?

3. Expectations can be an indirect way of demanding something you want from someone without having to ask for it or making an exchange. Do you do this? An expectation can also be an unstated agenda that you're imposing on others. Do you do this? Now ask yourself what it feels like when others use expectations to demand something of you or use them for their own agenda.

4. Decide whether you want to make releasing expectations an active part of your mindfulness practice. If the answer is yes, then start to release some of the small expectations that you hold. And then gradually start to work on the larger expectations that you are really attached to.

5. Turn the spotlight of mindfulness on your expectations of yourself. Are you burdened with self-expectations? Do you treat yourself harshly when you fail to live up to the expectations you have for yourself? Did these inner expectations come from others, such as your parents, or from your fear of not being good enough? Understanding the sources of your expectations can be clarifying, but remember that the way to escape their ill effects is to identify them and let them go.

Chapter 6

Balancing Priorities

One of the primary ways values and intentions manifest in life is through priorities. We create priorities based on the things that matter most to us. They give direction to our life. They help us set appropriate goals and rank them so that in any moment we know what we're about and what we want to accomplish. They also help us allocate time and resources, organize activities, and make decisions. Knowing your priorities, remembering them under pressure, and acting from them are essential skills for living authentically.

You undoubtedly have numerous immediate and long-term goals you hope to accomplish in your life, as well as tasks you'd like to undertake and activities you'd like to do. Realistically, you're probably not going to get everything done that you want to, so it's essential, if you are to experience a sense of fulfillment in life, that you know which goals or tasks take precedence in any given moment. Also, each day you are faced with situations that require you not only to take action but to choose those actions from a range of possible responses. If you are to retain a meaningful relationship to life, especially during difficult times, you will need a clear sense of what's most important for you.

Lack of clarity about priorities can be a major source of emotional chaos. When you don't know your priorities, you're prone to succumbing to whatever entices you in the present moment, even if it doesn't help you achieve what really matters to you, or to letting others determine how you spend your time. And if you have a number of professional and personal goals but you haven't prioritized them, you will inevitably encounter conflicts as you try to achieve them all. Over time these conflicts can be devastating to you and cause pain for those you hold dear.

A case in point is Steve, a Life Balance client, who came to me for help in deciding whether to sell his business. After a few months of working with me, Steve realized he had higher priorities in his life than running the business he had built and that he wanted the freedom to devote himself to them. He decided to accept a buyout offer from a larger company, but to my dismay he negotiated a selling price that was contingent on the future performance of his company. Once the incentive was in place, Steve became attached to making the earnout and didn't leave the company as he had planned. So instead of freeing himself from responsibility, he became an employee of the new company and ended up with even less control of his priorities! It was a nightmare for Steve; the new owners had different values and ignored his input in key decisions. In the end he made less money than he would have received in a straight sell and lost three years of his freedom in the process. During those three years, Steve would occasionally seek my counsel, but I could not succeed in helping him realize that it might be better for him to walk away from the company and get on with his priorities. His fear and anger with himself over making a bad decision kept him in such a reactive mind state that he simply could not let go.

In contrast, another Life Balance client, Jenny, came to me for help in sorting out her priorities after hearing me state in a lecture, "Just because you're good at something doesn't mean you have to keep doing it." Hearing this had been liberating for Jenny. As a college student she had worked hard and achieved national recognition. After graduation she went on to become a star in her profession, the person everyone admired and sought out. After twenty years she was tired of feeling the pressure to perform. She wanted time to be with her young family and pursue other interests. What stopped her was the obligation she felt to the opportunities she had been given because of her talent. Whenever she imagined doing routine work rather than her "star performer" work, she felt she was being selfish and self-indulgent and that it was wrong not to use her talent. In just three sessions with me, she clarified her priorities, created a timetable for making the change, and identified the key steps for getting there. Then she did it—gave up her prestigious work, made the financial sacrifice, and created the time she wanted for enjoying her family.

Setting Priorities to Live By

Priorities fall into two categories: outer and inner. Outer priorities are those things you want to achieve or do in your life, and inner priorities are how you want to go about accomplishing those things from moment to moment. In other words, your outer priorities are about *doing*, and your inner priorities are about *being*. Both are important and must be continually weighed against each other and balanced according to your values.

In a sense your inner priorities are more important than your outer priorities because they help you determine your outer priorities, and they help you maintain your balance even when you fail to achieve your outer priorities. One way to understand just how important your inner priorities are is to reflect on how bad you feel when you violate your own ethical code (even if no one else knows you have) or when you hurt someone else while seeking your own gain. Is this feeling of disappointment in yourself worth it to you? Probably not.

Your values and intentions form the foundation of your inner priorities. So in setting inner priorities, you are specifying how you wish to feel inside no matter what you are doing. Begin by naming your values and intentions and reflecting on what brings you peace of mind and joy. Acknowledging that you are a work in progress, set reasonable priorities that are truly possible for you to live out in daily life. As best you're able, rank your inner priorities on a scale of 1–3, with 1 being your most important priorities and so forth. As you do this, you begin to see which priorities support others and that together they form a web of priorities that can help ground you in daily life, even in the heat of intense desire, anger, or fear. Through this process of ranking your inner priorities, you also begin to understand how to balance your priorities. For instance, one of your priorities may be to tell the truth about what you feel and think and another priority is not to cause harm, so you develop a habit of what in Buddhism is called *right speech*, which involves saying only what is true and only if it is useful and timely.

In setting outer priorities, reflect on what matters most to you in both your professional and personal lives. What are your ego needs? What levels of physical comfort and financial security do you require? How critical is having a sense of professional achievement? Do you need others to like you? Or is admiration or respect of others more important? How essential is being in nature or having time for your hobby or your art? As with inner priorities, you will discover that your outer priorities also form a network, with some supporting others. You may be pleased with some, shocked by others, while some priorities may seem like anomalies. For example, some people discover to their dismay that vanity is a priority for them and mistakenly feel that they must work to rid themselves of it. You will certainly encounter conflicting priorities. But at this stage simply acknowledge all your various priorities and weigh how each one feels to you, without judging whether it *should* be a priority. You can't discern which ones are best without first understanding the forces in you that are vying to be lived out. Moreover, an unacknowledged priority can later sabotage your chosen priorities.

Once you feel as though you've identified all your outer priorities, you can then start to sort and discard them. Let go of the ones that are the least critical, because you have limited time and energy. You are not trying to be perfect but rather to establish a set of realistic priorities that work collectively and that you feel neither ashamed of nor guilty about. Just as you did with your inner priorities, rank your outer priorities on a scale of 1–3, with 1 being your top priorities and 3 being nonessential but nice if you can find time for them. As you rank your outer priorities, you will begin to see how it's possible to strike a balance among them. For instance, if exercising every day and career advancement are both top priorities for you, you may realize that you need to get up earlier in the morning to exercise before going to work, and give up your less essential predilection for being a night owl.

Integrating Your Inner and Outer Priorities

The final step in setting priorities is integrating your inner and outer priorities into your life. There will be times when they are in conflict and you will need to decide which one is more important. For example, you may have to decide between pursuing an inner priority such as creativity and an outer priority such as financial security. If developing your artistic abilities requires many hours of practice and expensive instruction, you may decide that for now it's more important to put energy into work in order to pay your bills.

I can't tell you how many priorities to set; however, I will caution you that fewer are better because you can only be continually aware of a few. Also, if you set too many, you will increase the odds that conflicts between priorities will occur, which obviously defeats the purpose of setting priorities. Only you can determine how many priorities is a comfortable number for you to consciously work with.

Although these steps are intended to help you get started setting priorities, living from your priorities involves more than just thinking about them and creating a list that you memorize. It involves developing a *felt sense* of your priorities, continually clarifying them in your heart as well as your mind, and then living them out as best you're able. Sometimes you will forget them. In some situations you will not know what your priority is. At other times your priorities will be in conflict. Such uncertainty and conflict does not mean you have made a mistake; you are not doing anything wrong when this happens. Life is simply like this.

Obstacles to Living Your Priorities

In the Life Balance workshops I conduct, I usually begin by asking participants to create a list of their priorities. I then have them draw a pie chart showing how they apportion their time over the course of a typical week. Finally, I have them compare their priorities with their pie charts. More often than not, people are surprised by the disparity between the two. They discover that the way they spend their time doesn't reflect their priorities at all.

For instance, one man insisted that his family was his top priority, yet when he created his pie chart he saw that he actually devoted very little time to his family. When I asked him to make a pie chart that was more in line with his stated priorities, he struggled with what to give up. I then suggested that he needed to examine how he was approaching his family life. He kept promising his wife and children much more of his time than he was willing to give, which made them resentful, so maybe he should be more honest with himself and more realistic with them. If he was truthful, and delivered on what he promised, they might be less angry. In turn he would feel less guilt and less dread in relation to his family and, therefore, he would be more likely to spend more time with them. He immediately saw the wisdom in this approach and vowed to try and live it out.

In my experience, a disconnection between priorities and the amount time allocated to them is fairly common. Many, maybe most, people, even when they consciously set priorities, fail to live by them consistently. If this is true for you as well, understanding the reasons why can help you stay true to your priorities.

First of all remember that the you that's setting the priorities is actually a committee composed of different aspects of you—there's the you that's dedicated and caring, the you that's sometimes lazy, the you that gets in bad moods and complains about life, and so forth. Each of these internal committee members isn't necessarily interested in the priorities that were created by another part of you. Therefore when it comes to living out a particular priority, the whole committee isn't always in agreement and that priority loses out. When you're consciously trying to work out a conflict between priorities in some aspect of your life, it's useful to acknowledge the existence of the committee.

My advice in dealing with your internal committee is to be honest with yourself about your ambitions. It is not helpful to have an idealized version of yourself that keeps proclaiming what it really wants when there is an ambitious aspect of you that in fact makes the decisions in your life. You are not being authentic with yourself and that will eventually become clear to others. It is far better to compromise or to make a modest change than to go on proclaiming one thing a priority while doing another. There is nothing wrong with ambition—to be the greatest mother or father ever, to be liked by those who know you, to make money, or to accomplish something in the world. But you must then acknowledge your ambition as a priority and adjust your other priorities to include it.

A second common problem with living out priorities is that it's easy to lose sight of them because of emotional needs. This is what happened to Steve, the Life Balance client who sold his company but couldn't let go of the potential financial earn-out and get on with living out the other priorities in his life. Even under the least favorable buyout scenario, he was going to receive enough money from the sale of his company to never again have to work. However, he lost track of his priorities because financial insecurity was a major emotional weakness stemming from the poverty he experienced as a child.

It often happens this way—you don't realize that hidden priorities stemming from strong emotions are controlling you. I have seen marriages break up because one spouse had an affair and confessed their infidelity out of remorse and the other spouse could not find forgiveness. Only later did the injured spouse realize that their priority was not some ideal of fidelity. Their true priorities were honesty and starting over, not punishment. I'm not saying that you should always turn the other cheek in a relationship transgression; I'm simply pointing out that strong emotions occasioned by a particular episode do not necessarily represent your true priority. It takes time and reflection to ascertain what matters most to you. Then it takes periodic review and renewal to stay in touch with your priorities. This is yet another reason why being clear about your values and being committed to living from your intentions is so essential. When you mindfully live an intentional life, you stay in touch with your priorities and are able to feel when they have changed or you have gotten off course.

Old habits can also interfere with adhering to your priorities. You may have old habits that have nothing to do with your current priorities but are just as strong as they ever were. If you don't acknowledge these habits, they're going to win out over your priorities whenever your life becomes busy. Why? Because you don't have time to focus, so you revert to the level of your unconscious habits. For instance, you may set a priority of having better boundaries in your life, but when you come under pressure, the habit of pleasing others takes over and you never connect to your priority of saying no. However, over time, as you continue to mindfully work with your priorities, you will develop new habits based on your priorities.

Fear, even when it is irrational, can distort your priorities. For example, if you want to make new friends but have a fear of being rejected, you can never proceed. Time and again people will act out their fear in failed relationships, friendships, and careers. You can cease to have your fear be a limitation, but it requires mindful effort.

Oftentimes your preferences will overwhelm your priorities. You may want something that you know isn't a priority, but you want it anyway. For instance, you may volunteer for a start-up project at work because you like being part of everything new, even though you don't have the time for the project or any real interest in it. Or you may have a pattern of treating a particular preference as though it were a priority. For instance, you really dislike being uncomfortable, so you let this preference prevent you from being in situations where you could actualize a priority. Dieting and exercising are perfect examples of this trap. Many of us give in to our food cravings despite counting a healthy diet as being a top priority. The same goes for exercise—you know what you need to do to stay fit, but you don't do it because your preference is to not be uncomfortable. If you are mindful of the feedback life gives you in various forms of suffering, you can easily see where you are indulging in preferences at the cost of your priorities.

You may have priorities that are occasionally at odds with each other, and which make it impossible to carry out either one. In a situation like this, you may need to prioritize your priorities! For instance, you might want to do all you can to help out at your children's school, but you also need to take better care of yourself. If you keep trying to achieve both, you will accomplish neither well. Therefore sometimes you have to say "not now" to a priority or simply let it go. When you choose to let loose of a priority it may not feel good. In fact, it may hurt; the sense of loss or disappointment may linger for some time or return periodically. As with letting loose of preferences, letting go of priorities and mindfully bearing the loss gives you the strength and confidence to live according to your intentions.

Feelings of discontent or restlessness can be a sign that an urgent, unrecognized priority is trying to be heard. If it is really strong, then it may well sabotage your other priorities. A common example of this is being stuck in an unfulfilling job. For a number of reasons, you may need to stay in the job for a while; therefore you have to be creative in finding ways to satisfy your need for fulfillment, for instance, using the job to practice an inner priority.

Finally, you may have unrecognized ambivalence about your priorities. You may feel as if you're supposed to care about something, when in truth you don't, and make it a priority and feel proud about how dutiful you are being. But a priority that doesn't come from the heart isn't sustainable in the long run. It drains your energy and creates resentment, cynicism, and sometimes self-hatred. A good example of this is the story of one of my Life Balance clients, Sharon, a mother who did not enjoy doing a lot of what she considered to be "normal" parenting activities. She loved her twelve-year-old daughter unequivocally, and being with her one-on-one was a genuine priority. But she hated going to her daughter's soccer matches, taking part in her school activities, and socializing with her friends' parents. As a result Sharon found herself feeling ambivalent about parenting and questioning whether she should have ever become a mother. She was tormented by her ambivalence and felt so guilty that at times she became panicky. Her daughter was starting to act out, and Sharon feared that the child sensed her mixed feelings.

It took several Life Balance sessions before Sharon was able to admit the truth of her ambivalence, to accept it, and to realize that she had been trying to act in a way that she thought parents were supposed to act. After a lot of tears and being brutally honest with herself, Sharon determined that she was going to parent in her own way and in doing so would become a "great" parent. She withdrew from most of the social parenting roles, stopped spending time doing things with her daughter that she begrudged (like going to soccer matches), and instead spent it doing things that fulfilled her. While on the surface Sharon's decision may sound selfish, it worked out well. Once Sharon stopped trying to fulfill a priority that she did not have, her resentment went away, and she and her daughter grew closer. Her daughter is now a junior in college, very comfortable with herself, and quite sociable. Does this mean my client became a "great" parent? Probably not, but she did become an authentic mother, one who was empowered in how she loved her daughter.

Minding Your Priorities

Developing mindfulness is a top priority itself as you start your journey of living from your priorities. Mindfulness supports your journey in several ways:

1. It helps you initially as you explore your relationship to priorities to answer such questions as: "Do I have priorities?" "If not, do I want them?" "Am I good at living from my priorities?"

2. It enables you to observe yourself in daily life and assess whether the way you spend your time reflects your priorities.

3. It helps you assess how skillful or unskillful you're being in fulfilling various priorities.

4. It helps you begin to orient yourself from the perspective of your priorities.

As you become more mindful around priorities, you may encounter confusion, sloppiness, laziness, failure, and ambivalence, just like the people I describe in this chapter. The appropriate response when this happens is to have compassion for yourself. (Humor also helps!) The softening effect of compassion makes it possible for you to start over with renewed determination to live your priorities. In this way you build what I call *continual awareness* of your priorities.

Over time, and with consistent practice, you can develop a habit of continual awareness of your priorities. By "continual" I don't mean that you are mindful of your priorities every single moment of your life but that you periodically check in with your priorities—it could be daily for some and weekly for others—and reappraise them in the context of what's really going on in your life. You don't want to fixate on your priorities or cling to achieving them but rather use them as reference points as you go about your day. In doing so you enhance your sense of knowing what you are about and feeling authentic.

Assessing Your Priorities

Complete the following Life Balance Assessment in order to evaluate how well aligned you are with your priorities. The listed priorities are some of the most common, but you can come up with your own list instead. The first column is where you classify the relative importance of your priorities. The second column requires that you realistically assess how much time you devote to each priority. The third column asks you to reflect on the disparity between your priorities and the time you actually spend on each. For example, you may understandably spend too much time on an area that is a high priority, but it makes no sense to spend excess time on an area that is a low priority. It's also possible to over-allocate your time to a top priority and thereby throw off your overall time allocation.

LIFE BALANCE ASSESSMENT			
	Priority	Actual Time Spent	Analysis
	Rank by level of importance in your life 1. Very important 2. Important 3. Low priority	Indicate time allocation in your life presently √ Just right — Too little time + Too much time.	Select most accurate description A. Balanced B. I'm under-allocating time to this priority C. I'm over-allocating time to this priority
Career advancement			
Money			
Credit, glory, or status			
Power			
Time with family			
Intimate time with spouse or significant other			
Quality time with friends			
Personal time			
Health and fitness			
Psychological self-development			
Spiritual growth			
Making a difference or giving through service			
Time for leisure activities (dining out, listening to music, etc.)			
Time for hobbies and learning new skills			

Part II

Developing Skillful Behaviors

Now that you have begun to clarify what is essential to you and are familiar with the four practices that will empower you to live from this understanding, you are ready for the next phase of your journey. This part of the book presents skills that will allow you to manifest your values and intentions throughout your life. Chapters 7–9 describe life skills that clarify the mind, while chapters 10–12 address what I call *skills of the heart*. The last two chapters, 13 and 14, focus on life skills that naturally evolve from developing the capacities of a clear mind and a peaceful heart.

Chapter 7, on *starting your day with clarity*, looks at how your waking thoughts condition your day. If you develop a habit of renewing your intentions when you first wake up each morning, you'll find that it's much easier to live by them throughout the day. Chapter 8 examines how the tendency to interpret every experience gets in the way of *knowing what's really happening* in the present moment, causing you to react unwisely. Fortunately, there are steps you can take to avoid getting lost in the stories that your mind creates about the events of your life. Chapter 9, on *making skillful decisions*, addresses the chaos that arises when your mind lacks the clarity to make wise choices. It offers a step-by-step process for coming to a decision in any aspect of your life.

Chapter 10 describes two skills of the heart, *loving-kindness* and *compassion*. Loving-kindness and compassion can bring relief from emotional chaos and help you be at peace in the midst of pain and turmoil. Chapter 11, on *gratitude*, explains how an attitude of thankfulness frees you from being identified with the negative aspects of life. Chapter 12 reveals how *generosity* toward others can help you overcome your attachment to wanting life to be a certain way, which is often the source of emotional chaos.

Chapters 13 and 14 present two more life skills that you gain once you have developed the skills of mind and heart described in the previous chapters. The first of these is *doing the right thing*. Chapter 13 examines the unconscious motives that can undermine your intention to act skillfully at all times and offers instructions for building your capacity for doing the right thing. In the final chapter in this section, you learn to apply your newly acquired skills to *making major life changes*. In the journey from emotional chaos to clarity, it is very likely that you will feel the impulse to make changes in one or more aspects of your life. But unless you are clear about your intentions, you risk creating more emotional chaos. All the skills you have learned thus far will empower you to move forward with clarity.

Chapter 7

Starting Your Day with Clarity

There is one mindfulness practice that you can start straight away, with very little effort or investment of time, that can immediately enhance your ability to live from your intentions and priorities. I call this practice *starting your day with clarity*. If you give this mindfulness practice just five to thirty minutes after you wake up each morning, while you're still lying in bed, you can dramatically improve your sense of well-being and reduce the amount of emotional chaos in your life. You may be skeptical and think this sounds too simplistic, but if you give this practice a try, you'll quickly discover that the period of time just after waking up in the morning provides a rich opportunity for developing new habits of mind.

Think about that moment when you first wake up. You may not have even opened your eyes yet, but your mind is already busy. Almost immediately your mind begins to form an attitude about how you feel at that moment and about the day ahead. What your mind does right after awaking strongly affects you throughout the day; it creates the context for how you will perceive, interpret, and respond to all the things that will happen to you.

Your mind is fresher, quicker, more flexible, and less perturbed in those first moments after waking up than at any other point in the day. Therefore this is the perfect time for orienting yourself and grounding yourself in your intentions. You are less defined by your stories, less consumed by the soap opera of your life, and not so trapped in your persona. (This is the reason that spiritual communities consider the early morning hours to be ideal for prayer and meditation.)

Start with Your Body

The practice of starting your day with clarity begins with becoming mindful of what's true in your body and your mind when you awaken. So while you're still lying in bed, notice if you feel rested or if you're still tired. Is your body tense or at ease? What parts of your body are relaxed? Next observe your mind and notice whether it is relaxed or tense, quiet or busy. What is it doing? Is it resting, planning, complaining, rehearsing, or remembering a dream? It is fuzzy or clear? Is it experiencing an emotion such as excitement, dread, or fear? You now know what needs your attention.

The next step is to use your body or your mind state as an object of contemplation. Let's say that on a particular morning your attention is drawn to your body. Maybe you don't feel rested, or you feel rested but parts of your body are tense, or when you think about your day parts of your body tense up. All of these states are common. However, I've often heard people say they feel discouraged or inadequate if their body doesn't feel rested after a night's sleep or that if they realize they're tense in anticipation of their day, they feel guilty or ashamed. Even if your body feels fine, taking a few moments to appreciate the feeling can have a positive effect on your mind, and it can greatly enhance your ability to stay relaxed in your body throughout your day.

In response to whatever you discover to be true in your body, continue to lie in bed, and do a *body scan*. In a body scan you progressively tense and relax each part of your body as you imagine healing energy moving through it. You can start at your head and move down your body or begin with your feet and move upward. Some people like to visualize a feather brushing the various parts of their body. Invite your breath to move into those places in your body where you feel tightness, pain, or numbness. Not every part of your body will completely relax in response to the body scan, but most people report experiencing an increased sense of ease afterward. Sometimes while doing a body scan, you may fall back to sleep for a few minutes and wake up feeling fully refreshed, which was not how you felt before starting it.

If you have a high degree of emotional turmoil in your life or a great deal of pressure at work and wake up tense every morning, this progressive relaxation can help you release that tension before beginning your day. This in turn makes your day much more bearable and can even help you be more effective in dealing with challenges. When the body feels relaxed, the mind tends to relax and become more able to absorb the shocks that you encounter throughout the day. The difference this practice can make in your life is not trivial. One Life Balance client, who was going through a messy divorce and was afraid he would not get joint custody of his children, stated that scanning his body first thing in the morning broke the "locked in" feeling he had been experiencing for months.

There are several other benefits to doing a body scan each morning, including providing you with an opportunity to notice injuries in your body. Focusing on a particular part of your body where you have a problem and then inviting it to release can promote healing. And if you tense your jaw or clench your teeth during the night, focusing on your face, jaw, and neck can bring relief. One caution: when you aren't feeling well (if you have the flu, for instance), it is wiser to do loving-kindness meditation for your body instead of a body scan because you may become overwhelmed if you focus too much on your physical discomfort. (Instructions for loving-kindness meditation are given at the end of chapter 10.)

A body scan can also serve as a reminder of what you need to do to take care of your body or, mysteriously, provide you with an intuition about some part of your body that's asymptomatic but that needs medical attention. One morning while doing this practice, I had an intuition that I should go see a dermatologist, although no specific reason came to mind. I trusted my instinct and immediately went to a dermatologist. I described my intuition to the doctor and asked him to examine my entire body. He was skeptical, but he did the examination anyway and found a precancerous neoplasm near my spine. He said I was fortunate to have caught the malignancy at such an early stage and ceased being skeptical!

If you are dealing with a physical and/or emotional trauma that is either happening now or is a relic of your past, an early morning body scan can help you distinguish between the emotional disturbance and the physical challenge, which oftentimes are conflated. This discernment makes it possible for you to soothe yourself and calm your mind. Consequently you may find that your view of the trauma changes. Rather than it seeming fixed, you start to see your trauma as an event in the stream of your life that is characterizing your experience at this moment but that does not define you forever.

Creating a Relaxed Mind

Once you've completed your body scan, which can take as little as five minutes or as much as half an hour, turn your attention to what's going on in your mind. There are some people who wake up every morning with a sense of ease, quiet, and spaciousness in their mind.

For them, waking up is an enjoyable experience. However, most people more often than not wake up feeling tense, anxious, or even fearful. They become overwhelmed just thinking about all the things they have to do and begin to feel dread or antipathy toward the day ahead. Does this sound familiar? As you begin to notice what your mind does when you wake up, you may discover that you are caught in a pattern of looking for the difficulty that lies ahead in your day and making negative comments to yourself about what has to be done. This negativity creates tension and establishes a bad attitude. What an unskillful way to start your day! Or you may find that you wake up many mornings with a mind that's racing, jumpy, or out of sorts, and you may be accustomed to getting through this unpleasantness with the help of caffeine.

Notice too how your mind reacts to having either a good or bad night's sleep. If you slept well, you may take it for granted, never pausing to appreciate the good fortune of peaceful, refreshing sleep. But if you stay mindful, you will discover that a feeling of gratitude can be calming to your nervous system. If you had a poor night's sleep, you may feel sorry for yourself and complain internally. Be mindful of how this attitude toward your sleep affects you. Does the complaining, irritation, or frustration serve you in any way?

Now begin to focus on your mind, just as you did with your body. Is there underlying tension? Is it racing? Jumpy? If so, invite the mind to relax. You can evoke this feeling of relaxation in a number of ways: focus on a soothing memory or image, reflect on something you're grateful for, or do loving-kindness practice for your mind (see chapter 10). Over time the practice of starting your day with a relaxed mind helps create a new habit of maintaining a relaxed mind throughout the day. Another benefit is that you become more skillful at relaxing your mind whenever it becomes tense during difficult moments.

Imagining Your Day

After relaxing your body and mind as best you're able, the next step in starting your day is to contemplate what lies ahead. First picture the day in your mind. Observe your attitude as you imagine the various aspects of your day and the tasks you will be undertaking; it will shift dramatically depending on what activity you're focused upon. Likewise, you will notice different sensations in your body depending on which activity you're thinking about. When you focus on something that's difficult or requires a lot of attention, pause, breathe, and allow your body and mind to relax. Repeat this process of imagining, noticing, and relaxing until you feel centered. This feeling of centeredness becomes your reference point when you're actually engaged in the difficult activity you imagined.

Visualizing Your Intentions

After a few weeks of imagining your day and noticing how your mind and body respond, start to add the practice of remembering and clarifying what you are really about. While you're still lying in bed, invoke the intentions you are committed to living from every day. Imagine your day and visualize how you will manifest your intentions during your various activities. You don't need to go into a lot of detail; the purpose of this practice is to cultivate a general feeling of living from intentionality.

A few minutes of contemplation first thing in the morning can save you hours of tension and recrimination later in the day. Reconnecting to your intentions clears up negative, anxious, and resentful attitudes that may already be present when you wake up or that could potentially surface later in the day. If you are anticipating that a difficult situation will arise at some point during the day, you might imagine some of the ways you could become lost, anxious, fearful, greedy, or desperate and then visualize how you might respond differently from your intentions. Having just a moment's clarity about this "hot spot" in the early morning will be a major help to you when you are actually going through it later in the day. The situation won't feel so charged, and you're less likely to get caught up in your habitual reaction. Even though it is a challenging situation, you will be okay because you're grounded in your intentions and not grasping at a particular outcome.

The nature of the mind-body connection is such that if you begin to contract in response to a difficult situation, you will feel it in your body as fatigue, nausea, or tension. The practice of visualizing your intentions early in the morning can provide you with a technique for grounding yourself if you start to experience any of these sensations in your body. Wherever you are, whether it's your workplace or your home, take a few minutes by yourself to become aware of your body, relax it as much as possible, then remember your intentions.

Reflecting on your intentions doesn't need to take more than a few minutes, unless there is something major happening in your life that has you completely caught. In such a case, it would be wise to spend more time going back and forth between relaxing your body and remembering your intentions in that situation.

The point of this practice is not to visualize happy endings to the various activities in your day but rather to develop the capacity to meet them skillfully, with clarity and ease. The chances that you will experience a positive outcome are greater if you are focused on how you are engaged in the activity rather than if you are focused on the outcome. When your mind is relaxed and you are grounded in your intentions, you are more likely to find a creative or intuitive way to bring about a positive result.

Gaining Clarity about Your Story

A final reflection that you may want to incorporate into the practice of starting your day with clarity is mindfulness of your story. Because of your unique history, you have evolved a series of stories that you repeatedly return to throughout your life. These stories determine how you see yourself and how you interpret what is happening to you. Your stories can be so powerful that your life becomes a reenactment of them. As I described in chapter 2, you may well be overidentified with your stories and not see that they represent only one view of your circumstances. They may not have even come from you but may have been suggested by someone else.

The practice of starting your day with clarity offers an ideal opportunity for recognizing your stories and seeing the suffering they cause you. Your fresh mind can see them for what they are—just stories—and can watch them come into play in anticipation of your day. I'm not suggesting that you get rid of your stories but rather that you begin to recognize them as merely thoughts stemming from memories, associations, interpretations, and projections that you've strung together. Any given story might be true, might have practical implications, and may come from a genuine feeling of suffering, betrayal, or failure, but you do not have to be defined by that story. It is one of many things arising in your mind, and it is just something that characterizes the moment. If you pay attention to the story and don't cling to it, the amount of distress it causes you will be dramatically reduced.

I once worked with a middle-aged man who suddenly began to recall difficult childhood memories of his mother. He hadn't exactly forgotten the memories; he had always vaguely remembered that certain events had happened, but they were ideas in his head, like the stories he heard about his mother from other people. Then one day he suddenly started feeling what it was like to have those experiences. He would drop into these *felt memories* at random times throughout his day, and they would completely discombobulate him. I suggested that he try the practice of starting his day with clarity, focusing on body, intention, and story. I also encouraged him to practice brief versions of the technique at least twice a day and whenever he started feeling overwhelmed by his memories. He was so motivated by his fear of becoming dysfunctional that he was very disciplined in doing the practices. He soon started feeling as though he had some ability to affect what was happening to him, and over the course of a few months his sense of being a victim of these memories completely dissipated. He still had much psychological work to do, but he had gained the clarity with which to do it.

No matter how good your life circumstances are, you are affected by your stories. You may not even recognize them as stories; to you they may seem like worries or just the way you are. If this is the case, my advice is to be more curious and to look more closely. We all have stories about how the world is, how love works, what's possible in a relationship, what it means to raise a child, and so on. We even have stories of an *archetypal* nature, meaning stories in the *collective unconscious* that we share as humans. Your stories can limit what you believe to be your choices and define what happens to you in your day. As you gain clarity about your various stories, you gain clarity about your choices and what truly matters to you.

The simple practice of starting your day with clarity creates the momentum for you to connect the disparate events of your day into an integrated whole based on your intentions. Imagine the effect of a steady daily practice over weeks, months, or years. What new possibilities might open up for you if you indeed awaken each day with clarity? Isn't it at least worth a sustained effort to find out?

Cultivating an Attitude of "As Best I'm Able"

You can enhance the practice of starting your day with clarity by committing to and cultivating an attitude that focuses on your effort rather than on the results of that effort. I call it "as best I'm able" practice. The goal of this practice is to align your values with your words or actions as you carry out the tasks of your day.

1. Ask yourself if you truly want to make this practice a core attitude in your daily life, and if so, what it means to you.

2. Engage in this practice each morning by stating to yourself, "I intend to treat each part of this day as an offering by living it as best I'm able."

3. Throughout the day practice being mindful of your attitude as you do your various activities.

4. Remind yourself throughout the day that you intend for all your words and actions to arise from an attitude of "as best I'm able."

5. Notice when your attitude is one of judging yourself for not doing your best, and consciously remind yourself, "Even in these circumstances, I wish to do the best I'm able."

6. Be mindful of those times when you actually speak or act from this attitude, and acknowledge to yourself that you have lived out your commitment.

7. When others demand that you meet their expectations, respond by saying that you are doing the best you are able to do. Beware of making a false claim, and don't fall into the trap of using hindsight to redefine your best effort.

Chapter 8

Knowing What's Really Happening

After your morning practice of starting your day with clarity, you leave home for work feeling fresh, centered in your intentions, and knowing your priorities for the day. But before long things start to go wrong and you quickly lose your sense of well-being. The person sitting next to you on the bus is talking loudly on her cell phone, and you start imagining that she's doing it just to irritate you. Meanwhile your boss calls to tell you that he is canceling the project you've been working on for months, and you begin worrying about whether you might lose your job. Next your spouse sends you a text message telling you that he has to cancel your weekend plans because he needs to work, and you feel slighted because he didn't discuss it with you. You're already having a bad day, and you haven't even made it to the office.

What happened to the sense of well-being and clarity you had when you left home? It was hijacked by your *interpretation* of your experience. The difficult bus ride, the conversation with your boss, and the message from your spouse are all just experiences to be had and to respond to as skillfully as possible. They do not need to define your day. But instead of staying mindful of your intentions and staying focused on your priorities in each of these situations, you began to interpret each experience and then got lost in your interpretation, deciding that you could lose your job, that your spouse doesn't treat your relationship like it's a priority, and so on.

Notice how your interpretations put you at the center of everyone's life. The rudeness of the woman on the bus was directed at you; your boss's actions were aimed at you; your spouse's lack of consideration was all about you. Self-referencing is typical of interpretation and therefore can be a clue: when you observe your mind thinking in this manner, you know it's falling into interpretation.

At no point during that bus ride did your interpretations contribute anything positive. Your ability to respond skillfully to each situation was compromised by a thought or feeling that popped into your head and formed a view about what was happening. You abandoned your actual experience for untested, unreliable speculation about what might be happening. As a result you ended up feeling miserable and ineffective. It's sobering to realize that some version of this scenario may be going on in your mind every day.

The Difference between Experience and Interpretation

A crucial skill for minimizing emotional chaos and sustaining clarity in your life is the ability to distinguish between your *experience* and your *interpretation of your experience*. Your experience is simply whatever is happening in the moment—a sound, a taste, a bodily sensation, an emotion, any kind of interaction, etc. Your interpretation is your mind's reaction to that experience. One way to understand this difference is to picture that when you are directly experiencing a moment of life, you are *within* it; when you are interpreting it, you are *outside* it.

Interpretation occurs as the result of a combination of several factors. The mind has an automatic tendency to interpret an experience and create a story about it based on memories, past associations, and attitudes you have about yourself and others. It then selectively gathers data from within the experience to support its interpretation. It may seem to you that your mind is simply trying to figure out your experience, but really it's screening for evidence to support the story it's clinging to. However, this story is a delusion because your mind is being clouded by the strong emotions of the moment.

You can easily become committed to a particular interpretation to the point that it becomes a habit, a story that you repeat in similar or related circumstances. For example, "nobody wants to date me" is a story I often hear from both single men and women between the ages of forty and sixty. This belief is usually based on a very limited effort to make contact with potential partners that is undermined by unrealistic standards they have held since they were in their twenties. But when I point out that they're more mature now and may need to change their criteria, I am often met with an exasperated look that says, "You don't understand." They cling to their interpretation of the problem rather than allowing the challenge to evoke the change and inner growth that is necessary given the arc of human life.

How the Mind Resists Uncertainty

When confronted with a difficult experience, the untrained mind wants to be anywhere but in the present moment, where it perceives acute unpleasantness. The mind becomes anxious whenever it's uncertain and reacts as if one's survival is at stake. So rather than staying with the experience and determining the best possible way to relate to it, the mind jumps to creating a story that involves worrying about the future or judging oneself or others based on past experiences. This pattern of resistance to staying present in experience is an automatic response arising from the limbic brain as it detects threats. Ironically, the story imparts a false sense of knowing what's going on and therefore can seem temporarily soothing.

When we start to interpret an experience, the thoughts generated by our reactive mind become our primary experience, as opposed to whatever is actually happening that needs our full attention and considered response. Usually we continue on with the activity, but our attention is split or less than complete. Is it any wonder that we don't do our best under such conditions? And sometimes we just can't continue the activity. For example, Scott, a Life Balance client, suffers from what he describes as "shutting down" at work. Although Scott is a high-performing manager, whenever his colleagues critique his ideas, his mind starts spinning and he has to wait for the episode to pass. He reports losing two or three hours a week due to being "triggered." Scott interprets his peers' feedback about his ideas as a personal attack.

You too may have triggers that cause you to get lost in interpretation rather than staying present; you may even have a pattern of interpretation that shuts your mind down but have never realized it's happening because you are so accustomed to it. For sure, there are so many different experiences vying for attention in any given moment that in order to deal with what seems like an overwhelming amount of stimuli the mind rushes to interpretation to gain a sense of control. In reality, though, interpretation creates a false impression of stability. As you start to become aware of your patterns of interpretation, be kind and nonjudgmental toward yourself. It's not helpful to fall into self-blame or self-loathing, both of which are forms of interpretation.

Becoming Mindful of Your Experience

You can begin to break the habit of automatically interpreting every experience by practicing anchoring your attention firmly within the experience. Notice any physical sensations and emotions that are arising and observe the state of your mind. Is it racing, agitated, fuzzy, or clear? For instance, if you feel that someone has not lived up to an agreement they made with you, rather than contracting into an interpretation of them or their motives, simply stay with the feeling of what it's like to be let down by another. You might say to yourself, "I'm just going to be interested in this," and then watch what happens. Just be in the moment and let the experience form.

I realize that what I'm saying sounds easier to do than it often is, especially when the experience you're having is going badly. Staying with the experience can seem impossible if you don't know what to do or think, and it's getting worse. But everything you're noticing and feeling, even your resistance, becomes part of the direct experience. If the situation doesn't feel safe, you obviously need to respond as skillfully as you're able to avoid getting hurt. However, if you're willing to let loose of controlling the experience, there is a greater possibility that you will intuitively find a more skillful way to respond than what your pattern of interpretation might dictate.

For instance, when you and your spouse are having a disagreement and she's not being the way you want her to be, it can be confusing or threatening to you. It's a disagreement you've had numerous times before, and so you jump to your usual interpretation, to reassure yourself. Sometimes that may work, but it's unlikely, because what you're really doing is recycling the experience. What would happen if you just noticed what you're experiencing? "In this moment, I'm hearing her words. My heart is troubled. But my body feels comfortable. What else am I experiencing? I'm having this moment that's emotionally unpleasant. It's so unpleasant that my mind is jumping to interpretation and it's grabbing hold of it." Could you just stay with that experience and see what unfolds? Sometimes we feel so compelled to respond to a situation that we rush to interpretation. But do we really have to? What would happen if we didn't give in to the drama of the situation? Maybe if you paused your spouse would take advantage of the silence to say something unexpected that could shift how you respond and therefore establish a new way of relating to each other.

The next step toward breaking your habit of automatically interpreting every experience is to practice being mindful from moment to moment of the distinction between experience and interpretation. Begin to notice, "Is there a difference between my direct experience of what's going on and how I've interpreted it?" You'll need to practice noticing over and over again before you really start to know the difference. The more you're able to distinguish experience from interpretation, the more you'll be able to stay in the moment, the calmer you'll be, and the more choices you'll have for responding skillfully to whatever circumstances arise.

For example, you may have a habit of collapsing into interpretation whenever you receive any form of rejection. If so, first observe the thoughts that pop into your head. Then notice what you're actually feeling, physically and emotionally, right at that moment, and ask yourself whether you can stand to be present with those sensations. Most of the time the answer will be yes. Finally, examine your ego. Does it feel demolished, insecure, or angry as a result of the rejection? Is your ego doing the interpreting? Have compassion for your ego and appreciate that it just received a blow, but don't let its compensating interpretations define you in the moment. If you don't buy into the interpretations, they will eventually cease.

Releasing Your Compulsion to Interpret

Once you begin to recognize that interpretation is only your view of an experience, it becomes possible for you to begin to release your compulsion to interpret every moment. Ideally, your goal is to create a new habit, a new default setting for responding rather than reacting to all types of experiences. Establishing this new habit starts by staying with the experience. When you find that you've jumped to interpretation, just notice the difference. The noticing gradually becomes automatic. There are many activities in your life that you do automatically—driving, cooking, typing, etc.—and that you more or less notice without noticing. In the same way, you can develop the habit of automatically noticing the difference between your experience and your interpretation of the experience.

When you discover that you are interpreting rather than staying with your experience, you don't have to stop doing it. I'm not saying that you must get rid of all interpretation, but I am encouraging you to learn to distinguish between experience and your interpretive reaction to it. As with any kind of mindfulness practice, being curious helps. Ask yourself: "What will happen if I practice noticing the difference between my experience and my interpretation of it?" "What does it feel like right now?" "How many times today can I notice? Twenty? Fifty?" Just be curious.

The opportunity to practice in this way occurs many times throughout the day and requires persistence. You may be in a meeting, driving your car, talking on the phone to a friend, or having a heated discussion with your child and notice the difference between your experience and your interpretation of the experience. The more you get used to it, the more you will notice it. The more you notice it, the more you will tend to notice it.

There undoubtedly will be moments when you won't be able to stay with your experience and you will become lost in interpretation, so it helps to reflect afterward. For instance, on your way home from work you might stop to pick up groceries for dinner. After leaving the store and driving halfway home, you realize that you forgot something. In that moment your mind becomes filled with frustration and you think, "My evening is shot. I either spend thirty minutes going back to the store or I heat up leftovers for dinner. Either way the family is going to be disappointed in me. How could I have forgotten? I'm so stupid!" At that moment you are being consumed by your interpretations and there's no stopping it. However, once you've resolved what you're going to do about dinner, you can then reflect back on what just happened. Imagine saying to yourself later, "So I forgot. I had this experience of forgetting, and then I had this interpretation of my experience. What was it like?"

You can also cultivate your ability to make this distinction by observing other people as they're acting out their interpretation of an experience or telling you about something that happened in their life. You can tell the difference between what actually happened to them and how they're interpreting it. I repeat: their interpretation isn't wrong, necessarily—it's just different from the real experience.

There are certainly times when you need to be able to respond to an event that's unfolding in your life while simultaneously interpreting it. For instance, you need to be able to interpret the body signals and emotional vibes of others in order to be a good communicator. Likewise, you need to be able to recognize and interpret patterns in people's behavior in order to be effective and anticipate change. Moreover, sometimes someone may harbor ill will or jealousy toward you or see you as a rival, in which case you need to take steps to protect yourself.

Remember Your Intentions and Priorities

You can really harm yourself when your interpretation of your experience overrides your intentions and priorities. Charles, another Life Balance client, is a good example of what can happen when you base your actions on misguided thinking instead of your intentions and priorities. Charles was a high achiever who was chosen to represent his company in negotiations with another company about how the two companies might collaborate on a project. In preparation for the negotiations, I helped Charles identify some crucial points that needed to be included in the partnership agreement. However, when during the meeting his counterpart at the other company suggested the same agreement we had defined, Charles responded by saying, "Let me think about it." When he told me this afterward, I asked him why he hadn't said yes on the spot. Charles replied that he didn't want his counterpart to perceive him as being too quick to agree and therefore weak; he also thought that there might be a chance of getting an even better deal. I was dismayed because what mattered was getting this particular agreement settled, and he had it in hand. But Charles got lost in his interpretation of what the other person would think of him and his ideas about how he was supposed to act in such situations. Sure enough, when Charles later contacted the other negotiator to accept the offer, he was told, "Since we didn't reach an agreement, I thought more about it myself and I no longer want to do it." Charles was devastated, but he learned a valuable lesson.

Showing Up for Your Life, Just as It Is

Each year at Spirit Rock, I help teach a daylong course in meditation for beginners, which hundreds of people attend. When you first learn to meditate, it's not unusual for your mind to decide that since you aren't doing anything else this is the perfect time to deal with your most challenging problems. The mind, therefore, can become quite agitated, so the students are given an opportunity during the day to have a ten-minute individual interview with one of the teachers, to talk about their experiences. A few years ago, a woman who interviewed with me presented a long list of seemingly unsolvable problems. I listened attentively as she described her difficulties, and when she finished, I spoke to her about the importance of practicing loving-kindness toward herself. As for resolving her problems, I had no suggestions other than that she focus on the experience of them and not on her interpretation of them. Recently the woman showed up at my weekly meditation class and said, "You won't remember me, but I am the woman you told to stay with my experience, not the interpretation." I did not remember her name or face, but I did remember her interview. "Well," she said, "those words were what I really needed. I now speak to all sorts of groups, and I tell them about that interview with you and give them the very same advice." She had learned to show up for her life by being willing to be present for what was difficult in her life. The same can be true for you.

Recognizing Story Patterns within Your Interpretations

When you get lost in interpreting an experience, it's usually a sign that you're creating a story. As you become mindful of your story making, you will begin to notice a pattern in the stories. Recognizing this pattern can free you from the habit of getting lost in interpretation.

1. Start to observe how often you create stories around your experiences. How many times a day do you create little stories around ordinary life experiences such as shopping or driving? How often do you create a bigger story when something unexpected happens to you?

2. Can you see how you have ceased to be connected with the actual experience once you've gotten wrapped up in the story? Pay particular attention to how you get ensnared by the story when the experience evokes strong emotions in you.

3. What are the common themes in your stories? For example, are you often being treated unfairly in these stories? Or are you being incompetent? Are you anxious, afraid, or worried?

4. Can you see how your story-making patterns reflect your view of life? For example, if you perceive that the world is a hostile place, then you may have a story pattern in which you blame others for your lack of happiness.

5. When you recognize that you've created a story, drop the story and just notice the experience. How does this change your mood, your emotions, or your feelings about yourself?

Chapter 9

Making Skillful Decisions

A significant source of emotional chaos in anyone's life is decision making. No doubt you have been faced with many decisions in your life and know full well how difficult it can be, at times, to choose between alternatives. The reason you may struggle with making up your mind is that you haven't yet developed skillful means for making decisions. Without a clear path for making decisions, you can easily lose your direction as you try to resolve issues in your life. You can end up totally avoiding a decision that needs to be made; you can freeze out of fear of making the *wrong* decision; you can become distracted by factors that are irrelevant to your decision; and, of course, you can make poor decisions. Once you lose your way, your mind becomes fuzzy and your willpower weakens, which leads to a lot of second-guessing about your decisions afterward. The consequence of all this emotional chaos is that often you are not very effective in implementing your decisions once you finally make them. The good news is that you can develop a conscious, deliberate approach to making decisions (both large and small), which will give you greater clarity in resolving and implementing your choices.

Do You Really Have a Decision to Make?

I often counsel students seeking help with making various life choices. The most common decisions they present are about whether to take a new job, have a baby, leave a marriage, take an ethical stand against some wrongdoing, undergo a medical procedure, or make a life change in order to dedicate more time to their spiritual journey. The two questions they most often ask may well apply to you: "How do I clarify my thinking when it is muddled by the stress of deciding?" and "How do I stay in touch with my deepest values when I'm feeling anxious?"

Before you can begin to make a wise decision, you first need to be real with yourself about the situation: is there a *genuine decision* to be made, or are you just postponing the inevitable? For example, one student, Gloria, came to me for advice about her job, saying she was thinking about quitting. As I questioned her, Gloria realized that her choice between staying in the job and leaving was not real. In fact, she was at such odds with her supervisor that there was almost no chance of her staying. Meanwhile her self-confidence was being destroyed. She came to understand that believing she had a decision to make was actually a way of avoiding the anxiety and fear of job hunting. By thinking she had a choice, and getting stuck on it, she was denying herself the chance to proactively seek new employment. Gloria was ultimately able to transform her avoidance into an active decision, and she now has a job in which she is supported and stimulated.

Another student, Alicia, also wanted advice about changing her life, but she was in a very different situation and faced a genuine decision. Alicia's company had just hired a new president, who valued Alicia's abilities and wanted her to take on more responsibility. But Alicia felt burned out and wanted more free time in order to explore her spiritual life. The problem was that she wasn't sure she could afford to quit and knew that if she changed her mind later she might not find such a great opportunity again. "Should I just hang in there a few more years, despite how I feel, or should I take the plunge, even if I regret it later?" she asked me plaintively. After many months of deliberation, Alicia decided to leave her high-profile job and now works for a nonprofit organization with a flexible schedule that allows her to pursue her spiritual interests.

Like Alicia, you too probably experience suffering in the form of stress, anxiety, and uncertainty when facing a genuine decision. However, it is possible to relieve the mental suffering you feel in connection with decision making by applying mindfulness.

Mindful Decision Making

Although I teach a number of skills to employ in decision making, they all rely on becoming ever more mindful of what is happening in your body, mind, and heart when you are making a decision. Mindfulness allows you to know what's true for you now, keeps you focused in the moment, allows you to stay real with yourself, and helps you overcome the many emotional and psychological issues that may arise when you are dealing with a complex decision. I call this approach *mindful decision making*.

Mindful decision making enables you to go beneath the surface level of your moment-to-moment life experience, which is clouded with emotions, to see the truth of what is happening. In daily life mindfulness helps you see clearly what needs to be done, what you are capable of doing, and how it relates to the larger truths of life. Applying mindfulness to decision making leads to clearer thinking and to staying connected to your core values, which is crucial to your peace of mind. There are three stages in the mindful-decision-making process that I instruct students to repeat until a clear decision emerges. I consider these three stages to be the basis for all skillful decision making, and they will serve you in any situation, including when you are participating in a group decision. If you learn to be skillful in making your own decisions, you will automatically become more skilled at facilitating group decisions.

Stage One: Come into the Present Moment

When faced with making a decision, first direct your attention to the felt experience of this particular decision. How does it feel in your body right now? Do you feel pressure? Anxiety? Does your stomach hurt, or do your eyes burn? Do you feel as though you've left your body? Often you don't notice what's really going on and miss the body's signals telling you what to do. By feeling the decision in your body, you connect with your intuition.

Oftentimes there is a vital piece of knowledge about the decision that your mind has not tuned in to but your body knows and is trying to tell you. For instance, one woman who came to me for an interview during a meditation retreat told me that she had said yes to a marriage proposal and thought it would be great but also said that she felt a "strange tension" in her body whenever she was with her fiancé. As she stayed with the feeling in her body, she was shocked to discover that she didn't trust her fiancé at all! After she left the retreat, she called off the wedding.

Next start to *name the actual decision you are making*, as best you're able, which will help bring it into focus. At first you may not be able to clearly articulate what the decision is. Other times you will be able to name it right away, but then change that description over time, especially if it's a big decision. For example, if you are weighing whether or not to stay in your current job, you may initially think, "I don't want to stay in this job because there's too much pressure," then a week later think, "No, I don't want to stay in the job because I don't like my boss very much." Another week goes by, and you realize, "Actually, I don't like the values that are involved in this type of work." By staying mindful of the decision over a period of weeks, you discover that your actual decision is whether or not you can work for a company when you are at odds with its values. You are able to see that it was the company's values that led to the creation of an unlikable boss and unbearable pressure. Therefore even if the boss left or the pressure eased, your unhappiness would not go away.

Naming may be the single most useful skill you can develop for decision making. By naming the question, you clarify it to yourself. You may be surprised at how hard it is for you to correctly name the decision in highly charged situations—no wonder you are struggling with clarity around it! I urge you to practice naming the decision even when it seems obvious what the decision is and even if you know what you are going to decide.

The act of naming alone can help release some of the tension around making a decision. One Life Balance client was offered a major job with the federal government and had spent many hours agonizing over whether to accept it, but was unable to decide. As we explored his dilemma, it turned out that he did not have a question about the job—he definitely wanted it—but taking the job meant that he had to give up his current lifestyle, which he was very attached to. He had been asking himself the wrong question. His decision was not whether to take *this* job, but whether he was willing to take *any* job that would require him to change his way of life. Naming the correct decision led him into a deep exploration of what he wanted the remaining years of his life to be about. Many valuable insights arose from this process for him. He recently told me that he now helps other leaders name the decisions that they are facing in their organizations.

Another important step in being mindful of a decision is to notice if you're *obsessing over the decision instead of engaging in making it*. If you are replaying the same thoughts over and over in your head, this is often a sign that you're avoiding making the decision. Your obsessive thinking means you are focusing on your fear of not getting it right rather than focusing on the decision. When you become mindful that you're just recycling your same old anxious thoughts about the decision, redirect your mind elsewhere. Often just noticing obsessive thinking and naming it will help you to stop obsessing.

Stage Two: Clarify through Investigation

After becoming present to your decision, the next step is to *clarify the decision through investigation*. First consider the scale of the consequences of the decision. There may be times when the long-term effect of a decision is minimal and you're getting distraught over something that's really not all that important. Or maybe it's not a genuinely hard decision; you just don't want to face it, and that's creating stress. Also, be realistic about the deadline for when the decision needs to be made. Are you becoming stressed about a decision that doesn't have to be made for a long time?

One Life Balance client kept bringing up a purchase decision in session after session, so I finally asked her how much money was involved in making this decision. I was surprised when she said fifteen hundred dollars. I pointed out that she made that much money in two days of work, therefore her anxiety about the decision could not possibly be related to money. As soon as I said this, her anxiety immediately disappeared. She then made the decision with ease. So what was her real issue? My guess is that she was concerned what other people would think if she made the wrong decision, and more important, she couldn't admit to herself that she lacked the confidence to make the decision. She had such a strong need to do everything right that it was a self-limiting attitude and caused her to exaggerate the import of her decision—it was just an opportunity for her to practice mindful decision making.

You learn how to make a right decision by making wrong decisions, and what matters most is that you stay mindful during and after the decision-making process so that you learn from the decision. If you are mindful in this manner, you will always receive a meaningful return from making a wrong decision, and sometimes it may be even more valuable than if you had made a better decision.

The next step in clarifying your decision is to ask, "What kind of decision is this?" (See "Five Kinds of Decisions," at the end of this chapter.) More than likely, you don't realize the nature of the decision you're making—you just experience it as pressure. Identifying what kind of decision it is can in many instances immediately ease your mental suffering or make the best choice obvious. For example, let's say you're trying to choose between two options that you're neutral about, such as moving to a new home, which your spouse would like to do, or staying where you are. You may well be getting tied up in knots because you think you're supposed to care a lot about the decision and be passionate about one of the choices. In fact, it's not that big a deal to you, so you relax and just let the decision go either way. But beware of telling yourself that you don't care when in fact you are avoiding the pressure and hard work of having to make a decision. Likewise, avoid saying to yourself, "Since my partner cares so much, I will just ignore what I care about and will just go along with whatever he wants." Both of these situations represent quitting on yourself and do not work out well in the long run. It's okay to allow someone else's preference to count more, but it is not wise to deny the truth of your own feelings.

You will also benefit by clarifying how others who are involved in the decision feel. Oftentimes, when you're making a decision that affects other people whom you really care about, you can become enmeshed in their feelings without realizing it. Or you may project what you think they want, which clouds your thinking. Simply restating the decision without a view to pleasing anyone else can help you discover what's true for you. One student took a job she wasn't all that thrilled about because every single person close to her kept telling her that she could not refuse such a great opportunity. Did she ever regret it!

It may seem obvious, but an important step in clarifying a decision is to determine whether or not you have all the information you need to make the choice. It's surprising how often people don't make the effort to gather all the information they need or don't organize the information in a way that facilitates making a decision. If you're prone to either tactic, it could mean that you're avoiding making the decision (or you may have developed lazy habits regarding decision making). Sometimes you discover that you are postponing a decision by claiming you need more information when in fact you don't, or find that it isn't possible to obtain more information; therefore you just need to go ahead and decide.

As you continue your investigation, ask yourself, "Why is this decision so sticky for me?" Your struggle with the decision may have to do with factors other than the question at hand. For instance, maybe you can't decide which house to buy because your real decision is whether or not you're going to stay in your relationship, but you haven't been willing to admit that to yourself. The decision about the house is an opportunity to face your true question, but will you? So often people don't; they simply go along rather than face up to the decision that truly needs to be made.

If you're facing a really difficult life decision and you can't embrace any of the options, you may be stuck because there's some inner change that needs to happen before you can make the decision. When I suggest to someone that they simply aren't sufficiently resolved *within themselves* to make a particularly difficult *outer decision*, I am often met with hostility, as though I were saying they weren't good enough. You too may feel that admitting to such a situation in your life is a sign of inadequacy, but it's not true. It simply means that you are being called to resolve a conflict between competing priorities or to clarify some ambiguity or ambivalence you have about the direction of your life.

The final step in clarifying your decision is to restate the decision and write it down on a piece of paper, along with what you perceive the inner and outer consequences of your choices to be. Cross-check your options with your core values and ask yourself whether they are aligned. You will be much more likely to feel at ease with your decision, no matter what the outcome, if you have made a choice based on your values.

Stage Three: Surrender to the Decision

Observe whether you're clinging to the idea of making the right decision. When you insist on a perfect outcome, you're only deluding yourself and procrastinating. Applying mindfulness, you'll recognize that there is no perfect outcome and that it's impossible to know what all the consequences of your decision will be, no matter what you choose. Consciously let go of your attachment to the decision being right. You're never going to know if you really got it right. It may be that it is the right decision for a while, but then it turns out to be wrong later; or maybe you made the wrong decision now, but it leads to making a much better one in the future.

As a further act of surrender, write down what your mind is telling you to do, then what your heart seems to want, and finally what your intuition seems to be saying. People are often surprised to discover that these three centers of knowing are in conflict and that the conflict is paralyzing them. My usual advice is to go with your heart and intuition, if they agree, but to do so utilizing the practical planning capability of the mind. One Life Balance client was trying to find someone to be the president of her company while she remained the chief executive, because she wanted to be able to spend more time away from the business that she had built. When she came to see me, she was on her second president, and he was frustrating her and making her paranoid; the first one had been a failure as well. When I asked her how she chose people for the job, she described a process that was very rational and primarily based on the candidate's previous experience. She had not allowed her gut to tell her whom to hire or let her heart say who would be fun to work with. It was no wonder her selections failed her. She resolved that she was going to let the current president go and choose a replacement that "felt" right to her.

Before implementing your final decision, you can try it on for a few days without acting on it, to test how it feels. Oftentimes valuable insight will arise from an imagined trial run. I describe this process of living with a decision as *acting as though it were true*. For this active-imagination process to work effectively, you must completely step into the reality that this choice is your final decision and there is no turning back. You hold to this pretense and maybe tell a few trusted people what you've decided, or perhaps write something to yourself about what comes next for you, or maybe interact with someone involved in the decision as if you have made your decision but don't tell them. After a few days of acting out your decision, the body may send you signals, or you may suddenly have a new perspective on the situation that hadn't occurred to you before. You may also discover heaviness in your heart if the situation isn't sitting well with you, or peacefulness if it's feeling good. I have used this process in making a number of major decisions, and it has helped me avoid making decisions I would have regretted later.

You're now as ready to make your decision as you possibly can be. The one thing you may not have done is to make the decision knowing that you have done so as best you are able and to surrender to living with the ramifications of the decision, whatever they may be. You will ultimately discover that it is not the decision but rather how you live it out that truly matters.

Even if the outcome of your decision is disappointing, there's still meaning in it because you were developing throughout the process of making it. You were being genuine and acting from your core values; therefore you've grown. You have more confidence in your decision-making ability, and others will feel this maturity in you. The result is that you will be wiser when making future decisions and more relaxed about the whole process.

Obstacles to Implementing Your Decision

When it comes time to implement a decision, some people freeze. They can't pull the trigger, say the words, sign the paper, or walk out the door. This may happen to you if you have trauma in your background, or have lost all confidence in yourself, or the stakes of the decision exceed the limits of your nervous system. At this point you may appeal to others to make the decision for you, which is seldom a good idea, and one that undermines your ability to make decisions in the future. Or you may frantically go around asking one person after another their opinion about what you should do and waffle after hearing what each person says. I've only ever seen poor results from doing this.

If you happen to freeze, don't feel ashamed or guilty; your paralysis is coming from impersonal causes and conditions. Eventually these conditions will change, and you will find the agency to act once again. In the meantime, you will have to bear the feelings of helplessness or inadequacy, so please do so with a compassionate and forgiving attitude toward that part of you that is immobilized. You are suffering enough from being in a freeze; there is no need to punish yourself further.

You can freeze up over decisions that have either small or large consequences, and it can happen when making decisions about work, relationships, or your inner life. What matters during this period of feeling immobilized is that you stay connected to your intentions and that you not abandon your goal to make a decision. If you're really paralyzed, I recommend talking about what's going on with someone you trust or a therapist; otherwise keep your mind state to yourself. I once worked with a young man who froze on the day of his wedding. It created quite a drama. But once I helped him feel that he could say no, he was able to unfreeze and say yes.

One last piece of advice: Making difficult decisions is hard work and there is tremendous uncertainty in it. It can be physically as well as mentally exhausting and can overload your nervous system. Therefore, when you are dealing with a decision, it is critical that you cultivate a nonjudgmental, forgiving, and kind attitude toward yourself throughout the process. Not only does such an attitude provide the calm space necessary for making the decision, it ripens these qualities, which are crucial for a meaningful and joyful life, within you.

Five Kinds of Decisions

Naming the type of decision you're trying to make will help bring clarity to the process.

Benevolent: All your options are good. For instance, choosing between two good job offers or between spending time with your family and taking a personal retreat. What seems like a benevolent decision can sometimes indicate a deeper, hidden conflict you are avoiding acknowledging because it's too unpleasant. Ask yourself, "Am I creating options for myself in order to escape facing a deeper issue?"

Neutral: You don't have a preference for any of your choices, yet you can't make the decision. This paralysis is usually a sign of a hidden conflict that's trying to express itself through the decision. Sometimes the conflict is with another person. The skillful way to handle a neutral decision is to be compassionate with yourself and mindful of how the decision feels in your body right now. Oftentimes the answer will reveal itself.

Mixed: There are gains and losses inherent in all your options, and it's not clear which is the wisest course. For example, the choice between committing to a relationship and keeping your independence; whichever choice you make, you have to give up something you desire. Beware of trying to have your cake and eat it too. Likewise be careful of fantasy decision making, such as telling yourself that although the person you're dating isn't really right for you, making a commitment will change him into a new person.

Undesirable: All your options have unpleasant consequences. For example, deciding whether to keep silent or speak out about a lie one of your coworkers has told, which will affect workplace morale. There's no good outcome, no matter what you decide, so it's a really hard choice to make. In this circumstance listen to your heart: ask yourself which choice will be the easiest for you to live with, despite what are likely to be unpleasant external conditions.

Unknowable: The consequences of the decision are unclear. For example, deciding whether to have a risky operation or an experimental medical procedure. It's a tough decision to make because you really don't know how it's going to play out. It's best not to make such a decision until you absolutely have to, and then clearly state to yourself the full consequences of making the choice versus staying with your current situation. People often underestimate the risks and downside of the unknown and exaggerate the negative aspects of the status quo.

Chapter 10

Cultivating the Qualities of Loving-Kindness and Compassion

Students in my weekly meditation class frequently come up to me afterward to ask how to work with the emotional chaos arising from difficult situations in their lives. Often it's about a personal failure or loss, or a problem they're having with a child or a challenging person. One woman recently confided, "I was so consumed by my work in my thirties and forties that I never really had a life. Now I'm fifty-two, and it's too late to bear children, and I'm probably never going to be with anyone." And a man in his mid-thirties told me, "I haven't done well compared to everyone else. I don't have much money, haven't really accomplished anything, and I'm alone."

Each of us has experienced the emotional chaos that arises from having failed to achieve our goals, or from being forced to live with continual physical or emotional pain, or from feeling hopelessly inadequate in regard to something or someone we deeply care about. Maybe you have to live with an irredeemable loss caused by a mistake you made or with the consequences of another's cruelty. What you may not have noticed is how you react to these losses, failures, and mistakes. If you look closely, you may discover that you reject the experience even as you're feeling it, never fully accepting it because you so desperately want something else to be true. I call this mental and emotional act of compulsively separating from what's true in your life *demanding a better past.*

Insisting that the past be different is a distorted and miserable way to relate to life, yet many people suffer in this way without ever realizing it. The more painful the feelings, the more likely they are to hold the experience at bay and never fully let it in so it can be processed and relinquished. Nor are they able to let it go, since that would require that they let it permeate them, to have whatever degree of impact it has for them. They separate from it by becoming angry or restless, or by shutting down, or they start to judge themselves or others and fantasize about how they could have been different or done things another way. They repeat this story to themselves over and over again and grow hard to the experience. Why? Because their pain seems so unbearable that to fully let it in would be to experience annihilation. They mistakenly believe separation is safety. Paradoxically, the opposite is true: allowing yourself to feel the loss is how you embrace life.

The Need to Self-Soothe

Demanding a better past is a coping mechanism that is part of a category of activities I classify as *self-soothing.* There are skillful ways of self-soothing, including seeking comfort from a friend, taking a day off to be by yourself, and getting bodywork, whereas demanding a better past is a form of unskillful self-soothing. Like everyone, you need to be able to self-soothe in wholesome ways when disquieting or disruptive things are happening in your external life or when your mind becomes severely agitated without any apparent external cause. If you don't develop skillful means for self-soothing, you may resort to unskillful self-soothing strategies such as abusing drugs, alcohol, food, or sex to comfort yourself. Or you will develop judgmental, paranoid, or fixated thinking patterns as a way to avoid feeling your emotions. The person who gets upset at the office and then goes home and picks a fight with their spouse is trying to self-soothe; they're just not doing it in a skillful manner. Likewise, the person who drives recklessly when running late or drinks too much or indulges in inappropriate sexual activity is also trying to soothe their pain, but doesn't know it.

The need to self-soothe is not a weakness. In fact it is a sign of maturity to be able to acknowledge this need to yourself. Whenever I teach the importance of self-soothing, there are always a few people (and they are almost always men) who will challenge me and argue that self-soothing is indulgent or that it's only useful for people who don't have their life together. That may be so, but I've observed that those leaders who can self-soothe tend to be long-term leaders, and that people in successful, rewarding marriages also have this ability. You have to be able to self-soothe in order to function; therefore claiming that self-soothing isn't necessary is like saying you don't need to breathe!

The Buddha taught that all humans are alike in their desire for happiness, no matter how unskillful they may be in searching for it. Self-soothing is a form of seeking happiness. In becoming mindful of the need to self-soothe, you discover skillful ways to collect, reassure, and calm yourself that restore your sense of well-being whenever you lose your equilibrium. The confidence you gain from knowing that you have the capacity to self-soothe empowers you to navigate life's difficulties with more ease.

Self-Soothing with Loving-Kindness and Compassion

When someone tells me about a difficulty in their life, I suggest that they can increase their capacity to self-soothe by using two Buddhist meditation practices, *loving-kindness* and *compassion*. Both practices involve clarifying your attitude toward what you are experiencing, which grounds you in the present moment and enables you to relate to the chaos in your life with a clear mind and an open heart. These two practices are equally useful in helping you receive and hold the pain and losses of other people, which is how they were traditionally taught.

In Buddhism the terms *compassion* and *loving-kindness* refer to qualities of the mind and heart as well as to specific meditation practices that can help you develop these qualities. *Compassion is an empathetic response to suffering* that allows you to be at peace in the midst of pain and turmoil. *Loving-kindness is the intention of goodwill* toward yourself and others. Together they greatly enhance your ability to stay mindful of your experiences, pleasant and unpleasant alike.

Compassion is an energetic movement of the heart, not a mental idea. It is what you feel when you see a small child fall and scrape a knee. Your natural response is to pick up the child, not because the holding can make the scrape go away, but because it provides a kind of comfort that is healing to the child's spirit. It is exactly this energetic spirit that you direct to yourself when you are fully accepting the truth of your own experiences. Energetically, loving-kindness is more proactive than compassion. It is not a response to fear or pain but rather a spontaneous feeling that wells up, an attitude of good will toward others that is independent of any particular condition.

In the type of Buddhist meditation I teach, there are specific practices for developing compassion and loving-kindness; the purpose of these practices is to cultivate the intention to embrace all parts of yourself and to overcome feelings of separation from yourself, as well as from others. You learn to receive and work with your faults, failures, and losses as sources of needless suffering and spontaneously move toward change in order to relieve that suffering. As these practices mature, you feel a sense of warmth, good intention, and deep sympathy toward yourself.

Compassion practice consists of repeating a kind of mantra, or prayer, to yourself: "May this suffering cease," or "May I bear this pain and suffering with ease." Another technique I teach is to visualize holding yourself as a young child and saying, "I can see that you are hurting, and I am very sorry. May your suffering cease." As you do this, you begin to experience compassion expanding in the body as feelings of warmth and well-being. Similarly, the practice of loving-kindness involves repeating certain phrases to yourself: "May I be well. May I be safe. May I be happy. May I have a life of ease." As with compassion practice, loving-kindness practice is about having the intention to accept yourself just as you are. (More detailed instructions for practicing compassion and loving-kindness meditation are given at the end of this chapter.)

Another factor that can help you cultivate the qualities of compassion and loving-kindness is the silence you can find in a meditation hall. Communal silence is like a magical elixir—it not only overcomes feelings of separateness between you and another but also brings together the separate parts of your own identity. The analogy of baking is sometimes used to describe this process. First you combine the dry ingredients—flour, sugar, salt, baking soda, etc.—then you stir in the water or milk. The addition of the liquid binds the dry ingredients together. Once they are mixed, the dry and wet ingredients form a dough. Then it is just a matter of baking with the proper amount of heat before you have a loaf of bread. In meditation the silence slowly mixes your various feelings, moods, and contradictory beliefs into a soft, pliable sense of presence, and the hours on the cushion produce the heat, which generates insight. It takes time for this heating process to work, but it doesn't matter if your mind is restless and constantly wandering or your body is in pain or you are filled with doubt; all these reactions are just fuel for your work on the cushion.

Opening to Love

Loving-kindness and compassion meditation are transformational when practiced over several years. They become established mind states such that you spontaneously respond to all situations with one or the other or both. When you reach this stage of development, you realize not only that you are capable of experiencing such beautiful mind states but also that when your mind is free of greed, aversion, and delusion it automatically generates these mind states.

As your capacity for compassion and loving-kindness grows, you also begin to discover the many nuances of love. Is love the same as desire? Is it love you are feeling when you wish good things for your loved ones? Or is love an unmoving energetic state from which all else moves, including your good intentions and good wishes? If it is the latter, then there is an unchanging state of love that we are sometimes in touch with and other times not. When you are in touch with this unchanging state, feelings of compassion and loving-kindness sponta-neously arise in you. You value these responses so much because they allow you to temporarily become part of this unchanging state of love. From this perspective, love is always present. It is we who are sepa-rated from this love due to our inability to simply be with things as they are. As you begin to stay more present, to fully receive the moment just as it is, you experience more loving intentions—even toward difficult people—because you feel less separation.

When I was first introduced to loving-kindness and compassion practices, during a ten-day silent meditation retreat more than twenty years ago, my reaction was to walk out of the room each time they were taught. I was interested in deepening my understanding of the mind, and when the teachers started discussing developing emotional qualities, I thought they were being sentimental. I was convinced one could not practice compassion as a discipline, and the idea of fostering loving-kindness through repetition of certain phrases seemed silly.

Moreover, since mindfulness practice involves not controlling the mind but learning to stay present with it wherever it moves, I thought what the teachers were asking us to do would interrupt the momentum of the practice. I was really irritated by the whole idea and felt resentment and distrust. I skipped the sittings in which these practices were taught and used the time to run on a nearby track, feeling simultaneously defiant and a bit guilty. After a few days of rebellion, it occurred to me that maybe I should have some actual experience of the practices if I was going to have such animosity toward them. So I started taking the instruction and, once I stopped feeling self-conscious, discovered that they had real value. The practices involve developing compassion and loving-kindness for yourself, your benefactors, those you are close to, and those for whom you have neutral or even negative feelings. I was amazed that they really worked.

Love Thy Neighbor and Thyself

We all struggle with how to find love for another, particularly a difficult other. Even more challenging for many is feeling love and acceptance for oneself. If you have self-hatred, it will define the quality of your love—or lack of love—and it will ultimately manifest in your love for others. You may protest, on hearing this, that although you struggle with self-hatred, your love for your spouse is mostly pure, and that certainly your love of your children is pure. I do not doubt the truth of your protestations, but experience has shown me that in the end there is only one love. Love is by its very nature unity, and if you have feelings of self-loathing, those feelings inevitably become part of your relationship with loved ones. They limit the fullness of the experience of love, both for you and the other. Also, if there is acute self-dislike, no matter how much you try to hide or ignore those feelings, they are injurious to those you love, particularly children.

Living with Regret

It is important to make the distinction between regret for your past actions or distress over present shortcomings and lack of self-love, which is experienced as self-loathing or feelings of worthlessness. These feelings of regret and distress are a necessary part of maturing. Of course it is appropriate to experience your faults for what they are, but it is even more important that you consider those faults in a context of compassionate love for yourself. As I pointed out in chapter 2, you can't create an authentic identity based on your faults; by acknowledging your shortcomings, however, you can see clearly the harm they cause you and others and avoid identifying with them. This clear seeing in turn motivates you to develop an inner life so that even the bad moments aren't wasted but instead become fuel for your growth. Moreover, fully opening to the suffering caused by unskillful behavior evokes feelings of compassion, the appropriate response to suffering, no matter its origin. Similarly, seeing that unskillful actions are the result of unhealthy mind states helps you understand the importance of compassion and loving-kindness practice in dispelling those mind states.

Reconciling the Past

Earlier I referred to the futility of demanding a better past, and indeed we become caught in a cruel cycle of suffering if we spend our lives clinging to such a misguided pursuit. However, we are not condemned to forever enduring a past full of painful memories and regrets. The past is not fixed in the mind; it can be dramatically changed by gaining new insights into it, by developing new attitudes toward it, and by holding it in the heart with loving-kindness and compassion. You can begin to redeem the past—whether it's something unfortunate that happened to you, some words you spoke (or didn't), or some actions you took (or didn't)—by accepting these events for what they are. You recognize that the past exists only as thoughts and associations that generate bodily sensations, as feelings of unpleasantness, and as words and images in your head. Therefore the past can be redeemed by how you relate to these thoughts. For example, if you were exploited in some manner, you can vow to never exploit others; if you never received praise, you can become someone who generously praises others; if you never felt love, you can be someone who celebrates the innate worthiness of others.

In making such a shift, it may help to picture your life as a piece of art—a painting or a musical composition—that is continually being created and the meaning of which resides in its wholeness. No single action or period of time is excluded from your work of art. But in the overall context of your intention to live from love, your past suffering becomes noble. It becomes material for creating meaning and value in your life. Your past may be awful and your life may be hard now, but suffering does not have to define you, even though it characterizes you at times.

When you have experienced great pain yet have a positive, ethical, loving attitude, you are an inspiration to others. If you were left physically or emotionally injured or constrained, your willingness to bear that limitation with courage becomes a testimony to the nobility of the human spirit. You are a reminder to others of what is possible. Likewise, if you've injured another person, when you consciously live with the truth of those actions, you give witness to the fact that every person is capable of such things and that we can choose not to cause harm in the future. You are living proof that we do not have to be defined by our worst moments.

As a self-reflective being who can imagine the past, present, and future, you have a gift that is unique among all known forms of life. But this gift must be mastered. If it isn't, your past suffering can run amok in your mind. Maybe this is happening to you at this very moment; you may be living a life of hidden despair (many highly functioning individuals do) or justifying your indulgences as entitlements in a meaningless world. In truth, your despair and indulgences are forms of collapse into neurotic or self-pitying suffering. You are worthy of living a more noble life than this. You have choice in what you make of your past—you can bear your suffering consciously and live with dignity, even in the face of great loss or difficulty.

If you wish to assess how you are relating to your own suffering, you can look at the strength and frequency of these four mind states in your daily life. First ask yourself if you are capable of compassion for yourself and others on a day-to-day basis. Next inquire whether you feel genuine happiness for the good fortune of others rather than envy or indifference. Then notice if you can feel loving-kindness throughout your day, sometimes even for those you don't like or who are frustrating you. Finally, notice if you are capable of consciously bearing moments of suffering with equanimity. When your mind regularly experiences these four mind states—compassion, sympathetic joy, loving-kindness, and equanimity—in daily life, then you are manifesting the highest form of self-soothing.

Loving-Kindness, or *Mettā*, Practice

In loving-kindness practice, you repeat the following phrases for yourself and then for your loved ones, friends, teachers, strangers, enemies, and finally all sentient beings. You can say these phrases either out loud or silently to yourself. Try to keep a steady rhythm going while you're repeating these words and avoid letting your mind wander. Visualize the person you're directing loving-kindness toward and how the benefits of each of these phrases would feel to them.

I developed the phrases below in collaboration with a group of inmates in a prison meditation program. The words represent benefits they could imagine in their circumstances. I encourage you to make up your own phrases.

May I be safe from internal and external harm.

May I have a calm, clear mind and a peaceful, loving heart.

May I be physically strong, healthy, and vital.

May I experience love, joy, wonder, and wisdom in this life, just as it is.

Compassion, or *Karunā*, Practice

In compassion practice, you respond to your own or another person's physical or emotional pain. Sit quietly, evoking the image of yourself or the other person, and repeat these phrases over and over again, allowing yourself to become open to the feeling. You can also practice compassion meditation for groups of people.

I can feel your suffering.

May your suffering cease.

Alternate phrases:

My heart is open to your suffering.

May your suffering cease.

Extended version:

I can feel your suffering.

May your suffering cease.

May the light of love and understanding penetrate the darkness of your pain (or your despair, regret, anger, or hatred, depending on the situation).

May your suffering cease.

May your suffering cease.

Chapter 11

Living into Life through Gratitude

Students leaving a meditation retreat will sometimes ask me to recommend a mindfulness practice they can incorporate into their daily routine that will keep them in touch with the experiences they've had during the retreat. There are many such practices, but occasionally I suggest one that often elicits surprise and sometimes draws skepticism: to engage in *the mindful cultivation of gratitude* every day.

Cultivating gratitude is a very powerful practice that balances your mind's tendency to focus on what's irritating or what's lacking in the present moment. Constantly focusing on the negative aspects of your experiences can lead to a distorted perception of life and undermine both your creativity and your sense of empowerment. Focusing on the negative also tends to flatten your experience of being alive and thus kills your joy and deadens the sense of possibility. Gratitude practice liberates your mind from this morass of dissatisfaction and helps bring clarity to your daily life. It is a particularly powerful antidote for the emotional chaos suffered by individuals who have depressive or self-defeating feelings and for those who habitually notice everything that's wrong in a situation.

Practicing gratitude with consistency leads to a direct experience of being connected to life, as well as to the realization that there is a larger context in which your personal story is unfolding. Cultivating thankfulness for being part of life blossoms into a feeling of being blessed, not in the sense of winning the lottery, but as a more refined appreciation for the interdependent nature of life. It also elicits feelings of generosity, which create further joy. Gratitude can soften a heart that has become too guarded, and it builds the capacity for forgiveness.

The practice of gratitude is not in any way a denial of life's difficulties. We live in troubling times, and no doubt you've experienced many challenges, uncertainties, and disappointments in your own life. Nor does the practice of cultivating gratitude deny the truth that old age, sickness, and death are certain. Rather, gratitude practice is useful because it turns the mind in such a way that it enables you to *live into life*. Having access to the joy and wonderment of life is the antidote to feelings of scarcity and loss. It allows you to meet life's difficulties with an open heart. The understanding you gain from practicing gratitude frees you from being lost or identified with either the negative or the positive aspects of life, letting you simply meet life in each moment as it rises.

Counting Your Blessings

There are numerous ways to use mindfulness to cultivate gratitude. Of course you acknowledge your appreciation when things are going well. But even more helpful is to notice those things for which you are grateful when you find yourself in a contracted physical or emotional state. I often instruct students to respond to a difficult situation by acknowledging it as such and then saying to themselves, "Yes, this is terrible, *and* I am grateful for . . ." For example, "I am angry at life's unfairness, *and* I am grateful I have a mind that knows this is so and can deal with it." Or "My back is killing me, *and* the sky is an incredible shade of blue today." I also encourage students to focus on the wonderment of nature and the human capacity for learning and creating.

It is so easy to become compulsively fixated on the terrible and tragic aspects of human life that you can forget that you ever had feelings of gratitude in the past. If you are prone to this kind of pessimistic view, I suggest you reflect on gratitude by inquiring whether it is time based. Ask yourself what has happened to all the gratitude you felt in the past. Where did it go? Do you believe that gratitude is dependent on feeling good right now? If so, isn't that a very small-minded, "what have you done for me lately" attitude? Doesn't it imply that your gratitude is contingent upon an exchange—as long as you feel good, you will be grateful, and if not, forget it?

You can also practice being consciously grateful to your family, friends, teachers, benefactors, and all of those who have come before you and have made it possible for your existence to be comfortable, informed, and empowered. Take a few minutes at the end of each day to mentally note the many people who have invisibly served you by providing medicine, shelter, safety, food, and education. You can appreciate all that you have received, even if it was given under less-than-ideal circumstances.

One Life Balance client, Russell, had been traumatized by his mother's behavior toward him when he was a child. When he told me his story, I understood why, despite lots of psychotherapy, it was still a dominant force shaping his life in middle age. During a meditation retreat, I introduced Russell to the practice of cultivating gratitude toward his mother. First I had him acknowledge all the vital support he had received from his mother, such as food, shelter, and socialization. Then I had him reflect on how fortunate he was to have been born in the first place, to have been born physically healthy, and to have been blessed with a good mind. Later, during a Life Balance session, he reported that he could now see his childhood from two perspectives and thus appreciate it in a new and more balanced way: Even though his mother had acted in ways that were abusive and even illegal, he was grateful that she had given birth to him and that she had blessed him with many good things.

To me this meant that Russell had achieved a certain degree of freedom from the tyranny of his memories, and we could begin to work at a more subtle level of gratitude. I asked Russell if he had ever behaved toward his own children or anyone else in the way his mother had acted toward him. "Never!" he said vehemently. "I would never act in such a manner!" I gently replied, "If that's true, then your mother gave you a clear appreciation for what values matter most to you, didn't she?" At first he wanted to deny this, but he couldn't. I went on, "Unfortunately, your mother could only teach you through her inadequacies and wounds, which meant that she acted in inappropriate, frightening, and hurtful ways. Her actions nonetheless gave you the willpower to not repeat her destructive behavior toward your children." He acknowledged that this was true. "So your suffering wasn't wasted," I told him. "You learned from it. It has helped shape your values and helped you develop strong boundaries. So why not be grateful for all that you did receive from her and grateful that you were strong enough to develop self-discipline and evolve clear values from the difficulty? Don't you think she would have preferred to be a better mother?"

By this point in our session, Russell was crying. Although he did not find complete release from being defined by his childhood, and to this day still struggles with his past, Russell reports that he has never fallen back into his old state of self-pity and helplessness. He says he can always find some amount of gratitude that prevents him from sinking into woe.

Gratitude Is a Steady Stream

If you were asked to make a list of things for which you are grateful, how long would it be? Twenty items, one hundred, five hundred? Most likely you would include your health, your mind's ability to function well, your family, friends, and freedom. But would it include the basics, like a safe place to sleep, clean air and water, food, and medicine? What about the earth itself, blue skies, a child's laughter, a warm touch, the smell of spring, the tang of salt, the sweetness of sugar, or that morning cup of coffee?

The meaning of such a list would not be to make you feel indebted but to clarify your understanding of the way life really is. It would be a reflective meditation that uses mindfulness to carry you beyond the superficial to a deeper experience of your life as it is unfolding moment by moment. By specifically acknowledging the good that in fact surrounds you, you learn to throw off the blinders of habitual assumptions that prevent you from perceiving the miracle of life.

The next step in gratitude practice is to actively notice things you are grateful for throughout your regular day. For instance, when you're stuck in traffic and it's making you late and irritated, you may notice you can be thankful that you have transportation and that other drivers are abiding by the agreed-upon driving rules, which prevent chaos and unsafe conditions. In other words, you are grateful that there is a level of well-being and community cooperation supporting you even in the midst of your bad day. You can do this not just once or twice but a hundred times each day. And you can do so not to get out of a bad mood or to be a nicer person, but with the intention of clearly seeing the true situation of your life. Traffic will remain frustrating, but the quality of the inner experience of your life unfolding will begin to shift. Slowly you will become clearer about what really matters to you, and there will be more ease in your daily experience.

Discovering the Web of Interdependence

A powerful gratitude practice that you can do right now is to reflect on an object in front of you—let's say a cup of tea—and acknowledge the thousands of individual acts of integrity and service that went into fulfilling your desire for that cup of tea. How many different hands touched your tea with care so that you would get to enjoy it? First someone planted the tea, and then the rain and sun nourished it. Then someone harvested the tea, someone else carried it to the market, where someone else bought it, and someone else shipped it to a warehouse where others received and packaged it and then shipped it on a boat that someone piloted. The boat was made by countless other hands doing skillful work. The tea arrived in your country, where someone inventoried and stored it in yet another building that was created by many others who were responsible for making it sturdy and safe. Eventually the tea was delivered to a store near you, where someone received and unpacked the boxes of tea and carefully displayed them on a shelf that was made by someone skilled at metalworking.

You went to buy the tea in a vehicle whose various parts were also created by thousands of people acting responsibly and with high standards, such that you trust the brakes to work, the wheels to turn, and so forth, and you drove on a road that was built and designed with care to accommodate vehicles like yours and drivers like you. You paid for the tea with money that you earned through an equally endless network of people being responsible.

You then returned to a home that was also built by many hands, using construction materials that resulted from the labor of thousands of people, according to standards that ensure your house will be sturdy and healthy. Feel the web of cooperation on which you are dependent! When you sip your tea, you are partaking of all this effort—all of these people, as well as the sun and the rain, are there in your tea. You are the beneficiary of this web of connectedness;

nothing exists by itself. All things are interdependent, even your body and mind.

The great Vietnamese Buddhist teacher Thich Nhat Hanh describes this interdependency by saying that we "inter-are." It's true that we inter-are. So much cooperation and benign and well-meaning behavior is occurring around us constantly that it can be a source of continual wonderment and gratitude.

I encourage you to go through this same reflection yourself using a different object. We are so conditioned to pay attention only to our aloneness and autonomy that we may never open up to this sense of mutual interdependence. I want to stress that realizing you "inter-are" does not diminish your autonomy, it creates a more realistic perspective that, along with creating gratitude, can bring ease to the mind's tension.

What Is Your Gratitude Ratio?

You might ask yourself about your *gratitude ratio*. Do you experience the good things in your life in true proportion to the bad things? Or do the bad things receive a disproportionate amount of your attention, such that you have a distorted sense of your life? It can be shocking to examine your life this way because you may begin to realize how you let yourself be defined by an endless series of emotional reactions, many of which are based on relatively unimportant, temporary desires.

When you look at how much griping you do versus how much gratitude you feel, you realize how far off your emotional response is from your real situation. The purpose of this inquiry is not to find fault in yourself but rather to motivate you to find a truer perspective. Why would you want to go around with a distorted view of your life, particularly when it makes you miserable?

I have one Life Balance client who compulsively notices only what's wrong in her life. She developed this habit as a child, as armor against a complaining and criticizing mother. Then as an adult she received a series of tough blows and so never outgrew her compulsion to complain. For instance, she recently got a new job, and when she told me about it, she only had negative things to say. In our sessions I use humor to help her see how selective she is in what she notices in her environment. I exaggerate her lamentations and compliment her on her amazing talent for seeing what's wrong with every single thing. My parodies make her laugh and loosen her emotional fixity. I also point out all the good things in her life and how she has grown. In most of our sessions, the armor that binds her falls away. It has been a joy to see her start to consciously know the warmth of gratitude. Recently she started volunteering at a nonprofit organization that serves people in distress, and to her amazement it brings her more feelings of gratitude than anything else in her life.

The Shadow Side of Gratitude

Without instruction, reflecting on gratitude can seem boring or sentimental, evoking memories of your mother admonishing you to eat all the food on your plate because there are starving children elsewhere in the world. Part of the confusion is that you may have come to equate gratitude with obligation. But real gratitude begins as appreciation for that which has come into your life. It arises out of this appreciation as a natural, spontaneous emotion. And it is often followed by generosity. When gratitude comes from feelings of indebtedness, by definition what's been given cannot have been a gift.

I once commented to a friend who had recently broken off a long-term relationship that he must feel a lot of gratitude toward his ex-girlfriend because she had clearly helped him grow in many ways. This comment made him furious, so much so that he started yelling at me. "I don't owe her anything!" he stormed. "What I've gained I got from working with myself!" I was completely taken aback. It would never have occurred to me to think he owed her something. Acting purely out of her love for him, she had shared her special capacity for intimacy with him, and it had helped bring about a major change in him. So he was the beneficiary of love, and by my reckoning this deserved a spontaneous feeling of gratitude. The only thing he "owed" was to utilize what he had learned from her in his next relationship. He could show his gratitude by passing it on in this manner.

Do you see how the old cliché about owing someone a "debt of gratitude" is actually misguided? *Gratitude is neither a debt nor an obligation; it is an attitude of appreciation that is so deeply felt in your heart that you spontaneously want to be as generous to others as others have been to you.*

There is a shadow side to gratitude, in which reality gets distorted in yet another way. This manifests as a hopeless or helpless attitude disguised as gratitude, and it expresses itself in a self-defeating, passive voice: "Yes, these things are wrong and unfair, but I should be grateful for what I have," or "At least we have this," or "Compared to these people, look how much better off we are." This voice, whether it is an inner voice or comes from someone else, is not to be trusted. Gratitude is not an excuse for being passive in the face of personal or societal need or injustice. It does not excuse you from working to become a caring person, creating a better life for your loved ones, or protecting the innocent. Acknowledging the great gift of a human life through gratitude entails just the opposite: it is a call to action to be a caring human being while acknowledging the folly of basing your happiness on the outcome of your actions.

Are You Shortchanging Gratitude?

Many students ask, "If experiencing gratitude feels so good, why do we often shortchange it?" If you can answer this question for yourself, you will gain valuable insight into how you make your life more difficult than it need be. Sometimes we shortchange gratitude because our mind is stuck in problem-solving mode; it only notices what isn't working and sets about trying to resolve it. This might seem desirable, but in fact there will always be things wrong in our lives. If we only respond to the negative, we reduce our experience of being alive. Is that what you want out of life? Do you really want to delay your sense of being alive while you await a perfect moment that is unlikely to arrive?

A second reason you might shortchange gratitude is related to the first: The mind tends to take for granted whatever is both desirable and present. This happens because the mind wants constant stimulation, and whatever is present and pleasant tends to recede into the background. It does not provide that stimulation. You can see this for yourself when eating a favorite food: notice how the first few bites taste so delicious, then how quickly the mind ceases to register the pleasant sensations. It is like this with everything—a cool breeze on a hot day, the sound of a stream as it flows over rocks, the freshness of the morning air after a rain. They all simply disappear from consciousness in the untrained mind. However, a mind trained in mindfulness of gratitude will stay attuned far longer and note more details of that which is good.

The phenomenon of *comparing mind* is another hindrance to practicing gratitude. It is the aspect of your mind that notices, "She has a nicer car than I do," "He is stronger than I am," or "She is a better dancer than I am." Understand that there is a difference between discernment, the factor of mind that sees things clearly, and comparing mind, which exercises judgment and hides a belief system that says, "If only I had more of the right things, I would be happy." This is a false belief, of course, a mental habit, really, but because it is unacknowledged and seldom examined, it holds enormous power in your life.

Unrecognized arrogance arising from a hidden sense of entitlement can also be an obstacle to practicing gratitude. When you have a strong feeling of entitlement, you don't notice what is going well but rather what is not right. This can stem from a sense of either having suffered unfairly or having been deprived. It can also arise from feeling special because you are smart, a hard worker, or successful. From the more subtle perspective of mindfulness, this arrogance reveals itself to be a form of ignorance in which these two truths are mixed together.

Finding Grace through Gratitude

The words *gratitude* and *grace* share a common origin: the Latin word *gratus,* meaning "pleasing" or "thankful." When you are in a deep state of gratitude, you will often spontaneously feel the presence of grace. Credit God, emptiness, Brahman, Allah, or the ground of the absolute, but the grace in receiving a human life is that it grants you the capacity to experience that which is beyond the mind and body. Reflect on this: you, with all your flaws, have been given this opportunity to consciously taste life, to know it for what it is, and to make of it what you are able. This gift of a conscious life is grace, even when life is filled with great difficulty and though it may not feel like a gift at the time.

When Henry Thoreau went into retreat at Walden Pond, he and his friend Ralph Emerson had been studying Hindu, Buddhist, and Taoist texts. He wrote: "I went to the woods because I wished to live deliberately, to front only the essential facts of life and see if I could not learn what it had to teach, and not, when I came to die, discover that I had not lived." He understood that conscious life was a gift for which the highest form of gratitude was to know it in all its depths.

This grace of conscious life, of having a mind that can know "this moment is like this," is the root of all wonder, from which gratitude flows. The wonder, the mystery, is that you, like everyone else, are given this short, precious time of conscious embodiment in which you can directly know life for yourself. However you find life to be— cruel or kind, sorrowful or joyous, bland or stimulating, indifferent or filled with love—you get the privilege of knowing it firsthand.

Gratitude for the grace of *conscious embodiment* evolves into the practice of *selfless gratitude*, in which your concerns slowly but surely shift from being mostly about yourself and those close to you to being about all living beings. As this occurs you need less and less in the way of good fortune. It becomes enough that there are those who are happy, who are receiving love, who are safe, and who have a promising future. It is not that you would not prefer good things for yourself, but your sense of well-being is no longer contingent on external circumstances. In a state of gratitude, you are able to rejoice that joy exists amid all life's suffering. You realize that pain and joy are part of a mysterious whole. When this state of selfless gratitude starts to blossom, your mind becomes more spacious and quiet, and your heart receives its first taste of release from fear and wanting.

"Gladdening the Mind" Meditation

Sit comfortably on a cushion or chair, with your spine erect. Take three deep, full breaths through the nose. Now notice any place in your body that feels pleasant. Keeping your attention focused on the pleasant sensation, allow the feeling to expand throughout your body.

As this feeling of well-being spreads, reflect on all the good fortune in your life, beginning with being born human and the gifts that come with having embodied consciousness: awareness of your own experience, the capacity to learn, and the ability to communicate with others in myriad ways.

Acknowledge gratitude to all those who have nurtured you throughout your life, starting with Mother Earth and including all the people who contributed to your development and sense of worth, from parents, family, and friends to teachers and spiritual guides.

Think of the many ways in which you've known delight in your body and mind, the ways in which your heart has been touched, and the ways in which you've touched the hearts of others. You are fortunate to have had this life experience, even though it has also been difficult at times.

As this gladdening of the mind ripens, stay connected to the feeling of well-being in your body. Happiness is the proximate cause of concentration. So as the mind becomes happier, your ability to focus becomes stronger; this in turn enhances the feeling of well-being. When your meditation ends, invite the feeling to stay with you as you go about your daily life, without grasping after it.

Chapter 12

Overcoming Attachments through Generosity

Attachment to having your preferences met or to achieving your goals is often an unrecognized source of unease and emotional chaos in your life. Of course you have preferences, and having wholesome goals is necessary for knowing your priorities, but clinging to what you want (which is what happens when caring deteriorates into attachment) does not help you attain your goals. Instead attachment creates tension, confusion, and anxiety in your mind—just the opposite of clarity. Therefore, in order to gain more clarity, it is essential that you cultivate an attitude of generosity. A heart that is filled with generosity reduces the tendency of the mind to become deluded by attachment.

I often encounter meditation students and Life Balance clients who take issue with the idea that attachment can be a problem. One mother told me of her heroic battle to get services for her special-needs child from the reluctant local school system and angrily proclaimed, "If I hadn't been attached to getting what my child needs, we wouldn't have gotten anywhere!" I respectfully disagreed with her, saying that it was her commitment that carried the day, not her attachment. You have to be committed in order to achieve your goals, to bring about change or to master a skill, and to keep going during hard times.

Commitment reflects your values, intentions, and priorities; therefore it fosters clarity. In contrast, *attachment is an unwholesome mental state in which you become overly identified with a desired outcome.* The more centered and free from grasping your mind is, the better able you are to sustain a commitment over time and to make clear decisions along the way. You're also less likely to cause harm in pursuing your goals. If you truly want to achieve something, be unswerving in your commitment to moving toward your goal but be flexible in your mind about the outcome.

Let's be honest. Most of our attachments aren't derived from lofty goals or heartfelt commitments. They're about feeding our ego, expressing our views and opinions, pleasing our senses, and being seen as we wish to be seen. Or they're about *not* being uncomfortable, *not* having to endure things that irritate us, and *not* feeling physical or emotional pain. All of this mundane attachment accounts for a great deal of the chaos in our lives, and it doesn't actually help us get what we want! It is pretty much a total waste of precious energy and a major cause of disquiet and unhappiness in life.

One Life Balance client, George, was so attached to getting the chief executive position at a prestigious company that he became a pushy, needy person during his interviews. I repeatedly told him that he had to let go of his attachment to getting the job, as he was creating a negative impression. But he couldn't, and unfortunately he wasn't chosen for the job. Afterward he was humiliated and distraught but much more willing to listen to my feedback that he had allowed his mind to idealize and inflate the importance of getting this particular CEO job and that it had undermined his ability to present himself well.

Attachments are so powerful because their formation is a critical part of your developmental process as a child, and as you age they become the dominating force in how you relate to life. But your attachments don't have to continue to control your life. Once you become mindful of your tendency to cling to getting what you want and the chaos it causes, you start to see that while you do have preferences, you don't have to be attached to those preferences. You then begin to notice that in many instances being attached to your preferences even gets in the way of actualizing them. Attachment leads you to become possessive, pushy, anxious, and overwrought, and your own chaotic mind becomes a hindrance to attaining your goals.

Mindfulness Techniques for Releasing Attachments

There are many mindfulness techniques for freeing yourself from attachments, including being mindful of your attachments and the suffering they cause (even if you ultimately get what you are attached to), and being mindful of the illusionary nature of attachments (you don't really want what you thought you wanted, or you did want it but now there's something else that's more important to you).

Besides mindfulness, Buddhism also teaches other techniques for overcoming attachment, such as renunciation. (In chapter 17, I go into more detail about renunciation practice.) In some Buddhist traditions, students receive training in ethics and generosity to free the mind from attachment *before* being taught to meditate. Being firmly rooted in ethics provides the discipline needed to overcome the temptation to act in ways you know are wrong, and it is an antidote to the tendency to rationalize unskillful behavior. Generosity is crucial because it balances the mind's tendency to grasp and become attached to people, objects, and outcomes. Instead of seeing the world from the perspective of what you don't have and desperately want, generosity allows you to view the world from what you do have and what you have to give.

Why the Beggar Begs

Practicing generosity is the intention to find release from attachment and egoism by giving freely of whatever you have of value. What you have to give may be material in nature or it may be your time, energy, or wisdom. Practicing generosity eradicates the attachment that comes from feelings of scarcity and separateness. Paradoxically, practicing generosity is also an act of self-liberation, yet it is not self-centered. True generosity arises out of unconditional caring and compassion for another. It does not mean self-sacrifice or recklessly giving everything away. Such acts are actually grandiosity disguised as generosity.

There is an old Sufi story about the importance of cultivating generosity, which asks the question, "Why does the beggar beg?" A seemingly crippled beggar sits in the central square all day, crying, "Baksheesh! Baksheesh! Who will give me baksheesh?" Some passersby ignore him, some give a little, and others give generously. He praises them all and asks that Allah bless them. At the end of the day, the beggar rises from his seat, walks over to the prayer fountain, tosses in the coins he has received, and then returns to his comfortable middle-class home. So why does the beggar beg? The last line of the story answers, "He begs for me and thee." This teaching asks you to reflect on how practicing generosity fits into your life and to be aware of the many benefits that accrue when you are generous.

The form your generosity takes is up to you, as it can only come from your values and what you have to offer. Remember it is your authentic intention that matters, even if it is simply a sincere wish that in time you will become more spontaneously generous.

Generosity means practicing generous behavior in all aspects of your life, not just giving money or sharing material possessions. Certainly the emotional impulse to practice generosity most easily arises when you participate in providing sustainability for others, whether it is shelter, food, clothes, or medicine. But with less immediate life needs, such as education, safety, or earning a living, the appropriate form of generosity may be a gift of your time. When it comes to intangibles such as justice and dignity, it may be most appropriate to voice your support. Generosity is, along with compassion, a cornerstone of mindful social activism.

In daily life generosity also means receiving each arising moment with a generous attitude and meeting it with patience. When interacting with friends or strangers, you give them your full attention as you listen to their words, and you interpret their actions with sympathy, even when they are clumsy. You cultivate magnanimous thoughts that allow you to see others in their best light and to interpret their actions as well-meaning until proved otherwise. Being generous in your thoughts doesn't mean that you're naive or that you permit a wrong action to go uncorrected. Rather, it means that you treat everyone as innately worthy of your respect and care.

A dear friend of mine died last year after a long and vigorous life. He had married three times, had raised four wonderful children, fought in World War II, mastered three professions, and through it all had always said yes to life. As he was nearing his end, his vitality deserted him and he could no longer say yes to life. About two years before he died, he said to me, "You know, I can't do much anymore. At first, it really got to me. Then I realized I can be kind to every person I meet. Say something true about their abilities or their smile, or thank them—something that makes them feel good. It's so satisfying." My friend had discovered the wisdom of practicing generosity, and it was his final way of saying yes to life.

You do not have to wait until you're vulnerable to be generous. The practice of generosity will invigorate you, lighten your load, and help you participate in the mystery of life. Generosity in any form is generosity; it nourishes the very essence of the other's being. In cultivating our sense of self-worth and well-being, we are just as dependent on the kindness of others as we are on our material needs. The deeper lesson is that each of us is equally dependent on others for our blessings. We are all interconnected with one another and with the earth in a web that goes beyond the marketplace of commercial exchange. We flourish or perish together through interwoven acts of generosity arising from the benevolence and integrity of people we shall never meet. This too is the power of generosity—even when practiced without consciousness it arises and spreads. When you mindfully practice generosity, you come into contact with its joyful, healing power.

You know when you encounter someone with a generous spirit. You part feeling more alive and better about yourself. What is usually hard to imagine is that you can be that way yourself. Yet with the conscious practice of generosity, you are slowly transformed. This is the blossoming of the *felt experience of interconnectedness*. When this starts to happen, the practice of generosity becomes more spontaneous and less deliberate, and your difficulties with others become less personal. Mind you, your fears and wants do not go away; you just cease to be so identified with them.

You may well see yourself as too impoverished to approach life with generosity, but this is a misperception. Practicing generosity skillfully, be it material, energetic, emotional, or in sharing wisdom, will only make your life richer. You can start practicing in small ways, with people for whom you feel appreciation, then gradually spread your generosity to neutral people and situations, and you can save the difficult opportunities for when you have built some momentum in the practice. It is not unlike doing loving-kindness practice. At first your generosity comes from your desire to be such a person; then it evolves into a more heartfelt experience.

One Life Balance client, Andrew, was very generous to the people who worked for him. He praised them often, nurtured their development, and patiently endured their shortcomings as long as they were committed to their own development. Andrew's problem was that he felt no such generosity toward his peers. He was envious of their successes and tended to be competitive and defensive around them. As a result he wasn't getting the support he needed from his peers to move to the top level of management. Moreover, his work life was becoming less and less fun since he was being excluded from meetings and not being listened to. I praised Andrew's generosity toward those for whom he was responsible and asked him to view his peers with the same empathy—to see their potential, to help them develop it, and to be patient with their shortcomings. And I suggested that he do this as a practice, not looking for a reward in the form of a behavioral shift among his peers. So Andrew started out by acting as though he had a generous attitude toward his peers without judging himself because he did not yet feel it. Gradually, through consistent practice, he began feeling truly generous toward them. This in turn enabled him to feel genuinely related to his peers. Within a year he was given a new opportunity that has led to the most satisfying work he has ever done. Today Andrew still has a tendency to fall back into ungenerous thoughts when he encounters someone who is uncooperative, but now he can remember his intention to be generous, adjust his mind state, and then respond skillfully to the person.

It is important to understand that mixed motives are to be expected when you practice generosity and that you are supposed to act from these mixed motives rather than wait to be inspired by perfect goodness. You practice generosity in order to recognize and move toward the purity that already exists within you. If you only had pure motives, there would be no need to practice! All that is called for is to practice daily in small but persistent ways—the practice will deepen by itself.

How Scarcity Limits Generosity

The opposite of generosity is the feeling of scarcity, which arises out of the belief that not having enough is the reason you're unhappy. "I don't have enough" and "If I just had such and such" are two phrases that reflect a mind state that is mired in scarcity. *The fear of scarcity inevitably manifests in symptoms of attachment—greed and envy—and is often accompanied by harsh self-judgment, insecurity, and a restless, worried mind.* "Scarcity of what?" you may ask. Scarcity of practically everything from money and other material goods to recognition and glory and even security against accidents or unwanted change. One may feel lacking in the attributes of beauty or sexual attractiveness, athletic or musical abilities, health, IQ, or technological savvy.

When scarcity becomes established in the ego you are increasingly susceptible to being overwhelmed by attachment. The Buddha described states of excessive attachment as mental "thirst." You can thirst after one sense pleasure after another and unknowingly organize your day around maximizing your comfort, which, ironically, creates more discomfort most of the time. You can thirst after particular outcomes related to your physical and mental abilities, your material rewards, your love life, and then any of the same for your children and others. Finally, you can thirst after wanting things to be other than they are. You may be *demanding* that you not be sick, lonely, childless, or financially challenged. The desire for something in your life to turn out a certain way and the demand that your life be other than it is are both forms of thirst that can create major emotional chaos.

Fear of scarcity has the effect of closing the heart, whereas generosity has the effect of opening the heart. Therefore practicing generosity shifts your attention away from what you don't have to what you do have, and away from yourself toward others. When you're habitually organized around getting what you want, you have an ever-present feeling of dissatisfaction; in contrast, cultivating generosity brings contentment.

Completing the Cycle of Generosity

There is a reverse side to generosity that is often neglected—the practice of receiving generosity. Many people are better at giving generosity than receiving it. It is a difficult practice that calls upon you to be both vulnerable and humble. My first great lesson in receiving generosity came long before I ever understood the word.

As a teenager living in the Appalachian Mountains, I worked as a bag boy in a local supermarket. To my consternation, it was the working poor who were most likely to give tips, people who often seemed needier than I. I would either refuse the tip or sometimes slip the money back into one of the bags as I put them in the car. I felt quite proud about this until one cold, rainy Christmas Eve when a man wearing cheap, worn-out clothes and driving a beat-up old car filled with many wide-eyed, unkempt children insisted on giving me a large tip. I was embarrassed at the idea of taking his money and flatly refused. He looked me straight in the eye and said, "This is something I can do for you. It is my Christmas."

Suddenly I got it—the tips were not about me; they were about the giver, his values, and his life. Unconsciously I'd believed I had the right to decide the appropriateness of another's generosity. Such arrogance! I accepted the money, deeply thanked him, and kept walking through the parking lot, pushing the empty shopping cart in the freezing air, rather than returning to the warm store. My ears burned from shame, but my heart was warm, for a generous spirit had touched me. I knew then that I had received a true gift, but it was years before I could make it my own. Being willing to receive graciously is another form of generosity. Without this willingness, the full cycle of generosity cannot occur. When we receive graciously, we are giving someone else the opportunity to be generous.

Cultivating a Generous Attitude toward Others

A pillar of practicing generosity is to have an *attitude of generosity* toward others. Anyone can develop a generous attitude, which takes many forms, including the following:

1. Being generous with your attention when you're listening to someone, regardless of how interested you are in what they're saying or how valuable it is to you.

2. Being generous when ascribing motives to a person's actions or speech.

3. Being generous when hearing another person's opinion. What I mean by this is that you initially assume there is some validity to their view, even if after listening to them you conclude there isn't.

4. Being generous in celebrating another person's happiness.

5. Being generous with your attention to someone who is lost, confused, or struggling emotionally.

6. Being generous in assuming that people are basically good (though of course you don't want to be naive or careless about how you interact with any individual).

7. Being generous with your sympathy toward someone who has experienced loss.

8. Being generous with your compliments and praise of others.

9. Being generous with your unconditional respect of others.

10. Being generous with your willingness to be helpful.

How Generous Are You?

Rate your capacity for each of these forms of generosity on a scale of 1–10, with 10 being the highest. Consider both your current capacity and the frequency with which you manifest each of these forms. If you want to increase your capacity, focus on developing one form at a time over a period of a week or a month.

Chapter 13

Doing the Right Thing

There are many sources of ordinary, or what I call *external*, happiness—happiness that's based on having conditions as we wish them to be. External sources of happiness include such things as a fine meal, beautiful scenery, and a nourishing touch. We also find happiness in favorable conditions—good health, sound sleep, feeling safe, etc.

Understandably, we feel fortunate if we have many moments of external happiness and regretful if there are few. However, we can also experience moments of happiness that are not based on external circumstances but that arise due to *internal* conditions. The Buddha gave numerous examples of this kind of happiness, including the happiness that comes from wise insight, loving-kindness, nonattachment, and right speech. The Buddha also spoke of the *happiness of blamelessness*, which arises when you refrain from committing harmful acts and when you act to do the right thing. (Oftentimes restraint and *right action* happen simultaneously.)

The sense of well-being that results from doing the right thing occurs here and now. It isn't dependent on having always done the right thing in the past but arises because you choose to do the right thing in your daily life. I don't mean to imply that committing to being blameless from this point forward will cause the burden of your past inappropriate actions to magically disappear. But once you become grounded in your intention to do the right thing, it can change how you relate to your past. For instance, you may become more capable of taking responsibility for the past and do so with much less self-judgment and inner turmoil.

By being mindful of your intention to do the right thing and then actually doing it, you directly connect with the happiness of blamelessness that the Buddha talked about. Each time you become aware of how harmonious it feels to be blameless, it increases the likelihood that you will choose to do the right thing in future moments.

The Happiness of Being Blameless

Whenever you do the right thing, your mind is clear and contented even though it may be conflicted. You may initially second-guess yourself, feel stupid for passing up pleasure, or feel anxious because doing the right thing may be dangerous. And it isn't unusual for your mind to still cling to the desire to get what it wants. However, once you have truly accepted your choice, a sense of ease arises in the mind.

There are times when I have counseled people to let go of a job or a relationship rather than do the wrong thing to get what they wanted. One woman, who worked in the health-care industry, decided to leave a job that paid extremely well because she did not believe in the efficacy of the product her company was selling. Even though she wasn't directly involved in sales, by playing a key role in the company she felt she was participating in something that was wrong.

A man who was just discovering the power of his critical mind was completely enthralled with a very attractive, younger woman. She would go out with him and afterward say that she didn't want to see him anymore; then sometime later she would indicate her interest in dating him again. It was maddening to him until the day he discovered that if he criticized her, her arrogance would disappear and she would collapse into insecurity and really want to be with him. When he came to me, he was distraught because he knew that what he was doing was essentially wrong and that it would not lead to a good long-term result. But in the short term, he got to be with her and she would seek to please him!

We discussed this on several occasions, and he defended his behavior by saying that if he didn't do this to her some other guy would. He rationalized that he cared for her and wanted to help her become more secure and maybe over time this would happen. I asked him to stop focusing on justifying his actions and tell me how he felt during and after criticizing her. Naturally, he said he felt awful and that he was feeling the cynical effects of his behavior in other parts of his life. And when I asked him if he wanted to be a person who behaved in this manner, he said no. "Then you have to do the right thing," I told him. "You already know this." And to his credit he did the right thing and stopped criticizing her. Not long afterward, she broke up with him.

In our first session after the breakup he was quite irritated with me; I understood why and let it be. I wish I could report that she later came back to him or at least came to appreciate how much he cared for her and wanted to be friends, but so far this hasn't happened. He says that he still has bouts of longing for her but feels as though he gained renewed respect for himself; therefore it was worth giving her up to do the right thing.

Doing the Right Thing When Lives Are at Stake

The stories I cited in the previous pages are examples of two people who experienced the benefits of choosing to do the right thing in everyday life, but the value of right action can be more fully felt in the story of someone who does the right thing on a heroic scale. For soldiers caught in the fog of war, the intention to do the right thing can bring a sense of clarity and transformation that results in heroism. A prime example of this can be found in the actions of Chief Warrant Officer Hugh Thompson Jr., a U.S. Army helicopter pilot, during the My Lai massacre. On March 16, 1968, Thompson and two crewmen were flying a reconnaissance mission over the South Vietnamese village of My Lai when they witnessed the slaughter of civilians taking place. Responding quickly to the senseless violence that was unfolding, Thompson set his aircraft down and rescued a group of civilians who were fleeing for their lives. When he returned to base, Thompson reported what he had seen to his superior officers. They in turn issued orders to the American troops in My Lai to stop the killings.

After completing his tour of duty in Vietnam, Thompson returned to the United States to train helicopter pilots. When the revelations about My Lai surfaced, he testified in a congressional inquiry and in the court martial of Second Lieutenant William Calley Jr., the platoon leader at My Lai and the only soldier to be convicted of the massacre. On the thirtieth anniversary of the massacre, Thompson attended a memorial service in My Lai. "Something terrible happened here thirty years ago today," Thompson was quoted as saying. "I cannot explain why it happened. I just wish our crew that day could have helped more people than we did."

Although most of us will never be called upon to do the right thing under such extraordinary circumstances as Thompson and his crewmen faced, we are challenged to do the right thing in numerous difficult situations throughout our daily lives. And although most of us are attracted to the idea of doing the right thing even when it's hard, we often feel inadequate. We're uncomfortable about whether we can find the way to do the right thing, or it's not clear to us what the right thing to do is. Sometimes we do the wrong thing because we're simply ignorant of what the right thing is; or we misperceive the situation; or our minds are clouded with greed, anger, or other emotions. But *if you are aspiring to live authentically, it is crucial that you make doing the right thing one of your intentions* and make it a daily practice. You can do this by setting the intention that "In this moment I'm going to do the right thing as best I'm able," and placing trust in your intention.

Trusting Yourself to Do What's Right

Trusting in yourself to do the right thing requires humility because frequently you're going to do the wrong thing, or your resolve to do what's right will prove weak, or your anxiety will be so strong that it distracts you from deciding what's the right action to take. For instance, how often have you been in a meeting at work or in a family situation when there's a so-called elephant in the room that needs to be named but you don't name it and neither does anyone else? Rather than judging and condemning yourself for not being able to do the right thing, simply accept that at the time you could not find the clarity and courage necessary to know what was called for and to act appropriately.

Similarly, there are times when you think you are doing the right thing but it turns out to be completely the wrong thing! Cultivating a humble attitude, accepting yourself, and taking comfort in the sincerity of your intention allow you to make mistakes and start over.

Yet another challenge to doing the right thing is that sometimes you simply don't know what is the right thing to do. When this happens, it's important that you recognize your lack of clarity, accept your situation just as it is, and embrace an attitude of *"don't know" mind*. With "don't know" mind, even though you aren't clear about what's the right thing to do, you have the clarity to recognize what not knowing what to do feels like. You may have to wait until you have more clarity or more time to decide what you think is the right thing to do. Under either circumstance, cultivating "don't know" mind allows you to avoid inner chaos and to stay balanced.

Even when you think you know what to do, humility is still called for because in reality you can't know for sure whether what you've decided to do is right. It's a relief when you stop clinging to the idea that you're supposed to know what's right in every situation or pretending to others and yourself that you know when you really don't.

"Don't know" mind prepares the ground for new possibilities to arise. When faced with a difficult situation, ask yourself, "Do I know for sure what's right?" If the answer is no, then do not take it as a personal defeat or a sign of your inadequacy; rather, have compassion for how difficult it is to proceed when you don't know what's right. This deep acceptance of your circumstances can actually help bring about clarity.

When Hugh Thompson landed his helicopter in My Lai, I doubt he was certain he was doing the right thing, although I think he knew he was risking a lot. His goal was to prevent more civilians from being killed, but they might have been killed anyway. His own helicopter could have gotten blown up, killing even more people, including himself and his crew. He didn't know what was going to happen. But in that fateful situation, his heart said, "This is wrong, and I'm going to stop this as best I can."

How Hidden Motives Trip You Up

So why is it so difficult to always do the right thing? First of all, you may be caught by unconscious motives. For example, you may be attached to the idea that you're a person who does the right thing. Although it's good to have the intention of doing the right thing, it's not so skillful to start identifying yourself as someone who always does. When you act from this identity, it becomes a kind of performance that's really motivated by your image of yourself. You will have a tendency to impose your idea of what's right on others, arbitrarily select which issues you champion, and ignore situations where you aren't doing the right thing.

Another unconscious motive that can interfere with your ability to do the right thing is what I call *false martyrdom*, an attitude that says, "I'm going to do the right thing, and then everybody's going to get mad at me for it." False martyrdom is actually a form of ego-tripping. People caught up in it are so attached to their views and opinions (without necessarily realizing it) that they alienate others and create an atmosphere in which it doesn't feel safe to explore what's right to do and how to accomplish it. They can't really participate in the process of learning, growing, and changing; in fact they sabotage that process by holding to their position so firmly that it brings progress to a halt.

Doing the Wrong Thing

The flip side of believing you're always right is to believe that you have a tendency always to do the wrong thing. There's no such person as one who always, or even often, does the wrong thing. Just like there's no one who almost always does the right thing. Although you may have a pattern of wrong behavior to contend with, each moment offers a fresh opportunity for you to choose the right thing. Negative thinking just gets in the way. It's just not useful in terms of responding skillfully to the moment that's arising.

You can also stumble when what starts out as a heartfelt motivation to do the right thing becomes an agenda. For instance, you might think you know what's best for somebody else, but you get so caught in your convictions that you try to force what you believe is right on them. When that happens, you've lost touch with your heart's sense of the right thing to do and have started to impose your view on others.

You may have become cynical about doing the right thing because you've done the right thing in the past and paid a steep price for it. You can also fall into the trap of thinking that you're supposed to be rewarded for doing the right thing. This is your ego wanting to take credit for something you did spontaneously from your heart because it was the right thing to do. Remember that you're not doing the right thing in order to be rewarded; you're doing it as a way of manifesting your intention.

When Hugh Thompson returned to the United States and testified in the My Lai hearings, he was treated by many of his peers as though he was the guilty party. When he'd go to the officers' club, the other soldiers would shun him. "I'd received death threats over the phone," he told CBS News. Thompson persisted in testifying, though, which created more enemies for him. However, he did not become bitter over the way he was treated. As he told the Associated Press in 2004, "Don't do the right thing looking for reward, because it might not come." This is a freeing realization. If there's no reward, then you're doing the right thing for the right reason. The real reward for doing the right thing is the right thing itself and what it feels like in the moment.

The Cumulative Effects of Right Action

Having the intention to do the right thing, even when it's difficult, has a cumulative effect. Each time you're challenged to do the right thing, and in doing so let loose of your attachment to your own well-being, you discover that "what doesn't kill you makes you stronger." In other words, it increases the possibility that you will do the right thing again in the future.

I used Hugh Thompson as a dramatic example of someone who chose to do the right thing in a big moment, when a great deal was at stake, but for you it's more likely to be the small moments in life that provide the opportunity to practice your intention to do the right thing. These small moments will help you strengthen your intention so that when a big moment arises, you'll be prepared to take right action. So in everyday life, practice doing the right thing when you're serving on a committee, or when you're deciding how you're going to split the housework with your spouse, or when you're listening to a friend confide her problems. Through this modest, humble approach, you'll slowly cultivate the potential that was always in your heart: to be a person who does the right thing.

Developing a Felt Sense of Doing the Right Thing

1. Can you recall three situations in your life that you now recognize as having been wrong actions? What clues did your body provide at the time? What was your mind state? Tense? Fuzzy? Jumpy? Buzzing? Start to be aware of such body-mind clues.

2. Is there someone in your life whom you admire for his or her right action? What seems to distinguish him or her from others? Imagine cultivating those same qualities in yourself.

3. Can you give yourself permission to acknowledge a moment of wrong action without collapsing into self-judgment or self-hatred? How could you develop a more compassionate attitude toward yourself when you do the wrong thing? Ask yourself if this compassionate attitude might help you to be more in touch with yourself and thus do the wrong thing less often.

4. Reflect on a couple of situations in which you did the right thing at some cost to yourself. How does it feel in retrospect? If it feels good, contrast that feeling with the uncertainty and hesitation you felt when deciding to do the right thing. This is why you can't trust the mind in a time of turmoil but rather need to rely on your deep-seated intentions.

Chapter 14

Bringing Mindfulness to Making
Major Life Changes

When you start to gain clarity through your values and intentions, don't be surprised if you suddenly begin to contemplate a major life change. You may discover that your goals are not truly aligned with your values, or that you now have a new set of priorities for your life, or that you've been profoundly unhappy in some aspect of your life for a long time but were afraid to face it. You may find that your situation is no longer acceptable and that you must do something to change it.

I often encounter people in just such situations in the meditation retreats I lead. During a recent retreat, one woman told me she was thinking of ending her marriage; a man reported that he was considering going back to his marriage, which he had left because his wife was having an affair; three people confided that they were contemplating leaving their leadership positions; and four people had already left their jobs and were looking for new kinds of work.

As you develop more awareness, you begin to have strong impulses to make changes in your life. This is normal! There's no reason for you to worry that you're going crazy or that you're being self-indulgent.

However, making a major change is a serious undertaking and needs careful consideration, reflection, and planning; and it needs to be approached slowly. To paraphrase C. G. Jung: with increased consciousness comes increased responsibility. For this reason, I and the other Spirit Rock teachers advise students as they leave a meditation retreat not to make any significant decisions until they have been home for at least as many days as they were on retreat.

Listen to Your Intuitive Wisdom

Sometimes your urges to make changes in your life are merely escapist daydreams or banal musings that shouldn't be given much attention. But other times these impulses are your intuitive wisdom speaking, and they deserve your full attention. Intuitive wisdom is a sense of knowing that's not based on conclusive data. It can manifest as a gut feeling, a sudden flash of knowing that comes out of nowhere, or an immediate recognition that something is right as soon as you hear it or see it. Your first task is to discern whether what you're feeling is a passing fancy or your intuitive wisdom calling for change. Mindfulness can help you consciously and skillfully allow this new, intuitive knowing to emerge, because it enables you to stay present with the intuition without interfering with it.

A perfect example of someone who learned to listen to her intuitive wisdom is Amanda, a Life Balance client who gave up being the CEO of a successful company to become an artist. When Amanda first came to see me, she couldn't name the impulse that was stirring in her, and it took five sessions before she could tell me that she had an intuition that if she did not leave her job it was going to kill her. She reported that with each passing year her work felt more and more challenging to her body and she felt less and less emotionally connected to what she did. Working long hours in a high-stress job was seriously harming her health, and she had been ignoring the symptoms for many years. Once Amanda accepted that what her intuition was telling her was true, she left her high-pressure position for one that was less prestigious but more fulfilling. Amanda's transition wasn't easy because it was hard for her to let go of all she had built, and she kept thinking that she was just being indulgent. Ultimately, though, her transition was successful because she had learned to trust her intuitive feelings and act on them.

In her role as a hard-charging executive, Amanda had been numb to the needs of others as well as her own. Interestingly, as she made her career transition she evolved into a more caring person. I have witnessed in other people this sort of profound inner change as a result of making an outer change. One Life Balance client, Alex, quit his job as the head of his family's business and as a result became much more empowered in his relationships with his family of origin and his wife. In Alex's first session, he reported that he enjoyed working with members of his family; however, in subsequent sessions he revealed a strong urge to leave the family company, even though it would upset his relatives. It was no wonder he felt this way. Despite being the one who created the profits in the family business, Alex had never escaped the role of being the "good son" who was compelled to appease everyone at the expense of his own needs. This same dynamic defined his relationship with his wife such that he couldn't voice his needs in the marriage. Alex listened to his intuition and left the family business; almost immediately he started interacting differently with his wife.

Such a seemingly unrelated change might also happen to you. You simply cannot know in advance the full effects of answering a genuine call for change in your life and responding skillfully.

Assessing Your Motivation for Change

Opening to the possibility of change is healthy: just as a plant loses its leaves or withers and scatters its seed, the old parts of yourself have to fall away, lie fallow, or die so that what wishes to emerge can do so. Mindfulness provides a method for consciously and skillfully working with the complexity of moving in new directions in your life. When an impulse to make a change arises, you should first ask: "What is my motive?" and then, "Is it wholesome?" A common example is weight loss, something a lot of people try to do, yet their motives are often unwholesome. For many, losing weight is a worthy goal because it promotes good health and ease of movement. But these health reasons are seldom the motivation behind dieting. Rather, it tends to be vanity or the desire for social acceptance. In such cases the effort put into losing weight is actually reinforcing the very longings that are throwing the person off balance in the first place.

Unwholesome motives will not help you move into a healthier relationship with yourself and seldom unify your efforts to change, so efforts to sustain your intentions fail and you never achieve your goal.

The same perspective applies to major life changes, such as shifting careers or ending a marriage. If you do not like how you are behaving in your work or your marriage, finding a new situation will seldom help. Your desire to escape is really coming from aversion to your own inner workings. On the other hand, if you are in an unhealthy environment or are being subjected to demeaning behavior, responding to an impulse to leave, even if it will mean much disruption, is healthy. So the same change or goal can be wholesome or unwholesome depending on the motive. That's why it's critical to spend time honestly exploring your motives before taking action.

One must approach major life changes with care and respect, for their consequences are far reaching and may create further unforeseen changes. One Life Balance client, Byron, who sold his business in order to devote himself to spiritual growth, discovered that he was not cut out for intense inner reflection. His challenge then became what to do with his time. He went through a period of being lost and feeling disappointed in himself. For two difficult years he was too prideful to seek help in dealing with his feelings, and he didn't want to admit to his family or close friends that he was struggling. When Byron came to me for help with understanding why his plan wasn't working, it was immediately clear that he was going to have to reassess his decision and make yet another change. By staying true in his exploration of his desire for growth, Byron ultimately fulfilled his intuition that he needed to make a change, as you'll see later in this chapter.

Exploring the Effects of Change

After assessing your motivation for change, the next questions to ask are: "What will be the results if I succeed in achieving the change?" "How will it affect my life and the lives of those around me?" "Will it really serve me, or at least cause no harm to others?" In my view, any change that does not yield more compassion and loving-kindness for yourself and others is a waste of precious life energy. It seems so obvious, but applying this simple ethical screen makes a difference in how wholeheartedly one can make changes.

Before committing to a major life change, you also want to ask yourself if it is truly needed. Is your urge for the new simply a way to avoid some inner work that you need to do in order to mature emotionally or psychologically? Are you trying to avoid a necessary surrender of your wanting mind? Is the change you're convinced you need really just an old idea that you've outgrown, or has it simply been unreal all along? Instead of trying to get more of something—money or attention, for instance—would you be better served by letting loose of your attachment to having life be a certain way? Each person has to go through this agonizing, self-doubting process as part of a major change.

Byron had made an incorrect assumption about his own maturity. He'd assumed that because of his considerable success as a corporate executive, he did not need any more ego fulfillment. But in fact he was lost without the day-to-day drama of carrying out business objectives, the attention of his peers, and the concomitant feeling of importance. He lacked sufficient self-knowledge to gain the clarity he needed to work through his inner issues. His situation was not made any easier by the fact that he was married to a woman who was quite successful and suddenly found himself being introduced as "so-and-so's husband." He had been wonderfully supportive of his wife, but his ego was not ready to handle this new identity in the world.

Skillfully Implementing Change

The next level of reflection relates to your plan of action. Ask yourself what means you should use to end the old and acquire the new. If the means for making change are harmful, then you are working at cross-purposes from the beginning, even if the motive and goal are benign. People so often panic at moments of change and act in a manner that is not skillful, hurting themselves and others as a result.

These hard questions are most alive when asked in the context of the spirit in which the change is to be made, which allows a deeper sense of meaning to emerge. Trying to get life arranged just as you want it never works. Looking back on my own life, it sometimes seems that whether I made a change mattered less than the fact that I grounded myself through this process of self-examination. Somehow, coming into my full range of feelings was the most important step toward continuing vitality in my life. And I've found that when I have failed to find this grounding in authenticity, I've paid a steep price.

It is not that you're supposed to be without mixed motives or never make poor decisions or be inconsistent in your behavior. Who is that perfect? You're likely to do all of those things. Rather, the idea is to be mindful of your intentions and behavior so you can make adjustments when you realize that you are off track. With practice you will become more and more skillful in responding to the significant changes that are needed in your life, whether you wanted to make them or not, and this is an immensely valuable skill to possess.

Life's difficulties aren't the cause of most suffering; rather, it's a lack of being connected to self, to others, and to life as a whole that leads to suffering. Separation from your natural enthusiasm dampens or kills your spirit. Therefore the question in contemplating change is always: "Am I moving more fully into my essence and into being my most authentic self?"

In changing his life, Byron didn't necessarily need to abandon his identity as a leader; he could have channeled it into leading a non-profit organization. In fact he tried being the CEO of a prominent charity, but he quickly became irritated with the organization's slow consensus-building process and quit. So what did he do to find peace? He returned to the corporate world he had abandoned. Due to his genuine talent, he was able to return successfully. To his credit, he is now, in his second round of being a leader, and as a result of his struggles, kinder to his employees, less obnoxious to his peers, and more socially responsible.

Sincerity, a Key Skill for Surviving Change

There are three lessons to be learned from Byron's example. First, sometimes you may make a change that turns out to be a mistake because you were confused about what was important to you, or you failed to understand all the consequences of the change, or you simply were not skillful in your implementation. Second, making poor decisions when undertaking a major change is okay as long as you're committed to learning from them. Third, sometimes you have to make the wrong choice in order to know what the right choice is!

Byron slowly grew in self-awareness. He stayed honest with himself during his time of being lost, he continued to recognize his ego needs, and he was mature enough to acknowledge his mistake. The result was that he did not simply fall back into his old patterns when he once again became a leader in the corporate world. Instead he became a more effective and caring leader who now knows what really matters to him.

Gaining self-knowledge was Byron's true transition. The major change his intuition was trying to lead him to make was really to become a more genuine leader. The same may be true for you. There's no guarantee that any change will unfold as you anticipate, but if you stay true to your quest, you will arrive at a destination that is of immense value to you.

Making Change Can Involve Periods of Darkness

Once you commit to making a major life change, be prepared to embrace some moments of darkness. They are part of that change. You are going on a journey, and it's natural that you will face difficulty along the way. Some of these difficulties will be due to external conditions—maybe you can't find another job, or your spouse doesn't support the changes you wish to make, or the economy crashes, or you have to contend with a health problem. And some of the difficulties will be internal—your unresolved psychological issues may arise in full force, your fear of doing the wrong thing may cause you to freeze up, you may lack sufficient self-understanding, or you may lose your confidence.

Creating ritual can help you navigate the darkness and transform the change into a sacred act. For instance, you might do any of the following:

- Surround yourself with reminders of what you are doing, such as objects or photographs of places or persons that symbolize your desired change.
- Read literature and poetry for inspiration.
- Enlist friends and professionals as both witnesses and as a support group.
- Write yourself a letter stating that you know you will make mistakes while implementing the change and that mistakes are part of the process.

It's important that you avoid judging yourself by whether or not you succeed in making a change, and never put yourself in the position of giving others the power to judge you on such a basis.

Let the act of changing be the reward, and do not count on a specific outcome, for it may be far different from what you imagined. All these steps represent a process of honoring yourself by surrendering the ego that thinks it is supposed to be in charge. They also honor the mystery of life, for no one ever knows the full consequences of an action.

As you reflect and make decisions about your future, never forget that the you who embarks on any life change will not be the person to reap its benefits or woes when the process is complete. Neither are you the person who made decisions in the past. You are only connected to the past by memory, by the consequences of cause and effect, and by the degree to which you embrace your life by owning your intentions. You are only here now, in this moment. Be alive to this moment. It is all you have, the only time when thought and action can occur for the benefit of yourself and those you love.

Assess Your Relationship to Change

1. Think about the times when you've made major changes in your life. Would you say that you're comfortable with change? Are you slow or quick to react when you realize there's a need for change? What about change makes you most fearful?

2. In which areas of your life (e.g., job, family, friends, relationship with your significant other) do you deal well with change and in which areas are you weak? Practice getting better at making change by choosing an issue from your area of greatest weakness and making it the focus of your mindfulness practice.

3. Begin to notice the truth that everything based on conditions is always changing. See for yourself that in daily life you navigate a constantly changing stream. If you persist, you will gradually feel more at ease with change.

4. How would you describe your parents' relationship to change? How much does your relationship to change resemble theirs? What values do you hold about change that you're not currently experiencing? What could you do to alter your relationship to change that would reflect your values?

5. Think back to a time when you were not skillful in dealing with change. Did you have compassion for yourself or did you judge yourself harshly? If the latter, did the harsh judgment serve you in any way? It is crucial to be able to discern when you are being skillful with change and when you are not. There is a difference between discernment and harsh judgment; can you feel the difference?

Part III

Removing the Sources of Chaos

The third part of this book looks at unskillful behaviors that are symptomatic of a lack of clarity and introduces practices that can help you overcome them. It begins with an exploration of how failing to establish and maintain boundaries can be the source of a great deal of chaos in life. Chapter 15 examines the different ways in which you may not be *keeping boundaries* and teaches you how to deal with boundary issues when they arise.

Without realizing it, you may be putting yourself under so much pressure that you are harming yourself. Chapter 16, on *ending the cycle of self-violence*, explores how you do violence to yourself by insisting that your life has to be a certain way for you to be happy.

The fear and anxiety that arise as you try to fulfill your ego's endless wants is another source of self-violence. Chapter 17 addresses how to free yourself from your ego's demands by *practicing self-restraint*. It outlines three renunciation practices that can bring you inner peace but don't require that you give up your material possessions or true aspirations.

Chapter 18 explores the chaos that results from ordinary compulsion—the urge to think, act, or speak in a habitual manner that deprives you of genuine choice in how you respond to life's events. This chapter details the various ways ordinary compulsiveness manifests and explains how you can *overcome ordinary compulsiveness* through a process of self-reflection.

The individual skills and self-knowledge that you have acquired thus far on your journey from emotional chaos to clarity have prepared you for the ultimate challenge: *living with the difficult*. Throughout life you are faced with difficult situations that threaten your sense of well-being. You now have the clarity of mind and heart to respond skillfully to the difficult so that you don't create yet more difficulty for yourself. Chapter 19 teaches you how to receive and be shaped by difficult experiences, including personal defeat, so you become a cocreator of your life instead of a victim of circumstances.

This section ends by asking you to free your heart and mind from chaos through practicing *forgiveness and reconciliation*. Chapter 20 describes how an attitude of forgiveness and reconciliation liberates you from the self-destructive forces of anger, hate, and resentment and gives you better access to your wisdom. The clarity you gain from engaging in these practices enables you to find meaning and harmony in any situation, even the most difficult or painful ones.

Chapter 15

Keeping Boundaries

Sophie, a professional in her midthirties and a student in my weekly meditation class, repeatedly feels taken advantage of. After listening to her describe a painful episode in which a friend acted inappropriately by going out on a date with her ex-husband, I told her, "You need to work on improving your emotional boundaries." She was surprised by my comment. "But didn't the Buddha say we aren't separate?" Sophie asked. "So why would I need to set boundaries? What am I protecting? Isn't the whole idea to not be attached to the needs of my ego?" Russell, another meditation student, revealed that he and his ex-wife, who share custody of their child, were working on boundary issues with a counselor. "We never worked this out while we were married," he said. "We thought being in love meant you weren't supposed to have boundaries."

I've had ample opportunity to observe that poorly defined or inappropriate boundaries are a cause of much suffering. Boundary issues are often hard to contain and spread to other aspects of your life. For instance, one woman with poor boundaries at work ended up being exploited by her coworkers. The situation made her feel so miserable that it affected her relationship with her long-term live-in boyfriend, who ended up moving out.

If you're struggling with boundary issues, you're in good company. After all, you're part of a culture that isn't always clear about boundaries. Moreover, your sense of appropriate boundaries changes dramatically as you mature and your wisdom deepens. Interestingly, in my Life Balance work with leaders and high achievers, I've found that they are generally good at keeping their own boundaries but aren't necessarily good at honoring those of other people. Also, despite usually being self-possessed, many of them struggle with maintaining their boundaries in some aspect of their personal lives.

Even if you've done a lot of psychological self-development work, you may still allow others to violate your boundaries or vice versa. You may have family, friends, or coworkers who chronically transgress your boundaries but have never realized it or repeatedly deny that they are doing it. Worse still, you may even be enabling their behavior. Fortunately, through mindfulness and intention you can dramatically improve your boundaries in a relatively short period of time, but it will take committed effort on your part.

Beware of underestimating the challenge of setting and maintaining healthy limits. Boundary problems aren't simply inappropriate language or intrusive actions, and their complexities are revealed only after you have gained some clarity about the nature of appropriate behavior and the power dynamics between two people. Mastering the issue of boundaries will not happen all at once; it's a gradual process that eventually leads to a more authentic and empowered you.

Evolving Boundaries

The language of personal boundaries mirrors that of property rights. The word *boundary* is used to define a parcel of land that can be bought, sold, insured, or taxed. Likewise, when used to describe emotional space, it most commonly defines the self, which has unique rights that others should respect. Abuse counselor Pia Mellody, in her book *Facing Codependence* (Harper San Francisco, 2003), refers to boundaries as "symbolic 'force fields'" that allow you to have a sense of self.

Today we take for granted the right to have our body remain inviolate, but throughout much of history many people—children, women, prisoners, serfs, slaves—did not enjoy that right because they essentially belonged to a parent, spouse, or ruler who possessed certain rights regarding their bodies. We now view a person's physical and even some emotional boundaries as innate and essential to their dignity and sanctity. This human right is considered more intrinsic than constitutional rights. But this view has only recently come into existence, not all cultures share it, and it continues to evolve.

It can take years for what may seem like an obvious personal boundary to be accepted as a civil right. For example, only recently has unwelcome touching by a boss or coworker been defined as illegal sexual harassment. It's still being debated whether the air around your body is protected and, if so, if you have the right to be protected, for example, from secondhand smoke. And now there's a debate about public cell phone use being an intrusion on our individual and collective space, a boundary that involves the right to peace and quiet.

Physical boundaries represent the right to be free from intrusion by others, and only when they are fully respected can emotional boundaries be dealt with. Violations of this physical right include torture of prisoners of war and criminals, rape, child abuse, and physical assault. In each instance there is also an undeniable emotional violation, which underscores the fact that emotional boundaries are as tangible as, and are fundamentally linked to, physical ones. Honoring physical boundaries is essential. The notion that the boundaries protecting against mistreatment of an individual's body are conditional, not innate, is a slippery slope that can lead to abuse by all sorts of violators, including police, governments, corporations, and those acting in the name of God. Eventually you and those you love would be affected. Any time our culture is complacent about such violations, all our personal boundary rights are threatened.

Opinion varies as to what constitutes physical violation in a given situation. In yoga class, for instance, one student may find the teacher's touch objectionable, while another doesn't mind at all. Given this lack of clear consensus about physical boundaries, it's no surprise that emotional boundaries are even more complicated. That means it's up to you to define and maintain your boundaries and to honor those of others.

If you're unclear about physical boundaries, you may have trouble developing reasonable emotional boundaries; you may engage in or subject yourself to verbal abuse, emotional intimidation, or intrusive behavior; or you may be inappropriately insistent or assertive. On a more subtle level, you may not realize that you have the right to psychological sanctity, that it's inappropriate for others to ask certain things of you, and that you have the right to say no to them. No wonder so many of us don't feel entitled to our own emotional boundaries—few of us have ever consciously explored them.

Crossing the Line

You may become entangled in two kinds of boundary issues: *trespassing* and *enmeshment*. Trespassing occurs when someone intrudes on your space without invitation or you infringe upon someone else's physical or emotional space. Inappropriate touching and invading someone else's privacy are both examples of trespassing. Trespassing tends to happen when there is an imbalance of power between two people. The more powerful person either feels they can get away with it or has an inappropriate sense of what they're entitled to, which is most often the case.

Many of the boundary violations that occur in workplace situations can be classified as trespassing. For example, your coworker, who is also a friend, repeatedly asks you to "help" her with her work, but she's really asking you to do it for her. A very common example of trespassing, although often not recognized as such, is inappropriate speech. When someone uses hateful or prejudicial speech or gossips about another person, they are violating the values of the other person. Although having your boundaries trespassed upon is disturbing, it's a problem that's easily recognized and that can, with goodwill, be negotiated. As you gain clarity about your values, you will become much better at maintaining your boundaries. People may try to bully or intimidate you, but your willingness to stand up and fight for your space will prevent further abuse.

Far more treacherous and confusing are boundary violations due to enmeshment, which is an inappropriate merging of identities. Enmeshment is *the failure to honor the psychological autonomy of another person.* This type of boundary violation may be one-sided or mutual—you and another can both become too enmeshed. Enmeshment issues happen most frequently in personal relationships, but they can also happen in work situations. For example, sometimes an employee will become so enmeshed in the company's success that they lose a sense of their own priorities. Many couples suffer from enmeshment. It can also happen in parent-child and sibling relationships, as well as between friends.

Enmeshment can take many forms: your spouse tells you what to think; your sister-in-law shares inappropriate details about her sex life; your mother corrects the way you speak to your children, in front of them; your best friend tells you whom you should date; your boss calls you at home to ask you to do the task he has neglected, assuming that his needs are yours to fulfill. In each instance, if you can't maintain your boundary, you acquiesce and are pulled into someone else's drama.

Enmeshment is prevalent in our culture. The concept became popular when psychologist Salvador Minuchin discussed it in *Psychosomatic Families* (Harvard University Press, 1978), a book he coauthored for use in family therapy. The term applies in so many situations because we tend to replicate the family dynamics of our childhood in most of our adult interactions.

Enmeshment gets even more complicated if you become codependent, either by inappropriately involving others in getting your needs met or by acting inappropriately to fulfill others' needs, thus robbing them of their independence. Because codependency is so widespread, many people are equally and mutually enmeshed, a situation that can be very difficult to change.

My student Russell and his ex-wife are a good example. Their feelings of love withered because each began treating the other as an extension of his- or herself. Unfortunately, intimate love is often misunderstood as a merger without boundaries. This phenomenon helps explain why you might divorce one person only to marry someone else who is very similar. Either this new spouse maintains better boundaries and the relationship works, or you re-create the same enmeshment pattern in your new marriage, which may eventually fail. Love is not sharing everything but sharing what fosters growth and wonderment. Love honors boundaries through restraint and not dumping your negative emotions on the other person.

Drawing the Line

You can learn to recognize trespassing and enmeshment, but avoiding or extricating yourself from them takes discipline and patience. To start I suggest using a four-step boundary practice in which you first recognize the feeling of wrongness, then reaffirm your boundary and acknowledge the truth of the situation, and finally act. (See the exercise at the end of this chapter.) This works for both trespassing and enmeshment, although for enmeshment you'll probably have to repeat these steps many times.

Enmeshment is insidious because you often feel compelled or imprisoned by it. You can't imagine doing anything but taking care of the other person. For example, you may have a brother, sister, friend, or adult child who repeatedly needs to be bailed out of one financial problem after another. You give them money, pay their expenses, and take over their debts, but nothing ever changes. You know that what you're doing doesn't work, but how can you refuse to help? As you become increasingly mindful of your role in perpetuating their problem, you realize that unless you set boundaries they're never going to take responsibility for their own well-being.

Although you may initially feel awful, once you've clarified your limits you'll feel much more authentic in your relationship. Sometimes your cohorts in enmeshment are better off as well; other times they simply move on to another codependent situation. Be careful not to do the same yourself and create yet another inappropriate situation—you may have a pattern of confusing codependency with feelings of love and caring. One Life Balance client went through a painful divorce from a woman whose behavior had forced him into a codependent role for years, only to turn around and marry another woman with the same issues! After more years of suffering, he divorced again. Now he's married to a woman with strong boundaries, who is very independent, and he finally has the love situation he sought for so long.

Problems arising from enmeshed boundaries are trickier to resolve than ones that involve trespassing, but both situations are subject to improvement. The discomfort you may feel when creating healthy boundaries is part of the journey; it tests the earnestness of your quest to be truly autonomous and to treat others as autonomous.

It is possible to develop a gut feeling about your intrinsic emotional and physical boundaries by being curious, staying mindful, avoiding self-judgment, and being compassionate with yourself. Healthy, resilient boundaries feed upon themselves—the more vibrant they are, the more they develop. Paradoxically, once you become strong in your boundaries, they become more porous, and love and caring flow more easily between yourself and others. In a fully mature state, your being can seem almost transparent to others.

Transcending the Line

This brings us to Sophie's question about why, if the teachings of the Buddha say we aren't separate, we need to set boundaries. This is an incisive question about a confusing issue. If Buddhism teaches that we are not separate, then why indeed should we worry about boundaries? Don't they create and even glorify the very self we're trying to transcend?

More than twenty-five years ago, psychologist and mindfulness meditation teacher Jack Engler addressed this question when he said that you have to have a self in order to let go of a self. This points to the importance of being mentally healthy—having a functional reasoning and integrating faculty—if you are going to develop the skills and insights that allow you to let go of greed and aversion and clear your mind of delusion. As Engler wrote more recently in *Psychoanalysis and Buddhism* (Wisdom, 2003), "It takes certain ego capacities just to practice meditation or any spiritual practice." Maintaining healthy boundaries is one such capacity. As Engler points out, it's a mistake to think that first you solve your ego problems and then you begin spiritual work. It's equally erroneous to think that if your ego becomes sufficiently healthy, your spiritual work will then be complete.

Psychological growth and spiritual liberation unfold separately and on different continua, but they can be mutually supportive.

Meditation practice can be very beneficial for developing your ego. Likewise, a healthy ego helps with the frustration, uncertainty, and pain of spiritual practice and greatly aids in transforming humiliation into humility. And at each step on the spiritual path, you still have to integrate what you've learned into daily life, which requires a healthy ego with good boundaries.

Beyond Boundaries

Through my own spiritual practice, I now see boundaries as being about *stewardship*, which means I have a responsibility for caring for my body and my mental and emotional states. If I'm a good steward, opportune conditions for both psychological development and spiritual freedom will arise, and I'll cause less suffering for others and myself. Good boundaries are not about me or my ego. Nor is there even a feeling of stewarding something that is specifically me or mine. There is harmony and possibility or there is not. Being a good steward likewise means showing the same respect for the boundaries of others. I may not always be able to experience boundaries this way, but that's my intention. Only gradually has it become a natural state, through repetition and habit.

I often urge meditation students to avoid thinking their goal is to get rid of their ego; instead their goal is to cease letting their life be controlled by the ego's wants. It's not your ego that causes your suffering; it's believing that life is all about meeting its endless wants. Of course it isn't easy letting go of attachment. You may experience a moment when you have ceased to be organized around the ego's demands and the ego reappears. What has changed is that you're no longer identified with it. You recognize that that ego is neither you nor yours.

Once you experience a degree of freedom from attachment,

you'll also realize that you still have a personality. You're simply not as caught in your desires or as deluded as before. You'll discover that it's possible to live in the moment instead of shrinking into thoughts about the past or the future, although you'll still have thoughts about both. You'll find that you simply *are*.

Four-Step Boundary Practice

1. Recognize

Practice being mindful of your emotions. This is how you learn to recognize when something is wrong or potentially wrong, even if you can't identify what it is. When you experience a major boundary violation, you may go into a kind of shock, feeling disassociated, confused, powerless, or at fault. This is your internal alarm going off.

2. Recollect

Recollection returns you to your physical body, to the moment, and to your own authenticity. To recollect, feel your feet on the floor, feel your hands, and find your breath. Making specific observations about these physical phenomena requires that you be present in the moment. Once you're in your body, you can feel the physical sensations associated with your emotions, which then helps you to be emotionally present.

3. Discern

Consciously acknowledge that a boundary is being breached and that you have the right to protect yourself. At this point you know that something feels wrong emotionally. You are present in your body, and you've confirmed that you don't have to feel this way. Sometimes you will be able to name the violation and other times you won't; you will just know that something is not right.

4. Act

Now you're ready to take action, to protect yourself, verbally or physically, as skillfully as possible. Mindfulness meditation is helpful in building your capacity to recognize and recollect. Therapy that uses mindfulness is also excellent in honing these skills.

When you act, it's essential to honor your own boundaries. What you do may or may not be effective in the moment, but you're changing how you relate internally to a pattern of external intrusions, and in the long run that's what will influence your self-esteem, effectiveness, and feeling of empowerment. This may mean walking away, changing the subject, or confronting the situation directly. It doesn't mean becoming self-righteous and persecuting those you perceive as violators. It's almost always better to protect yourself in the moment without assuming you're right; wait until you can clearly identify a pattern before you confront directly.

Chapter 16

Ending the Cycle of Self-Violence

I have devoted my life to exploring such questions as, given that life is finite and often difficult, how do we find meaning or happiness? Though they do not always yield answers, my explorations have led to certain observations about what makes life a struggle. One of these observations is how often we make life difficult for ourselves by being *self-violent*. Through the ways in which we schedule our time, push our bodies, and compare and judge ourselves against others, we repeatedly create an inner environment that is filled with violence.

Until this moment it may never have occurred to you that you are being self-violent, because your understanding of self-violence has been limited to physical abuse or other blatant self-destructive behavior that calls for a twelve-step rehabilitation program. Even now the word *violence* may sound too harsh to you, and you may reject the possibility that you could be harming yourself. But consider the dictionary definition of *violence*: "an exertion of extreme force to cause injury or abuse in the form of distortion or infringement." The extreme force can be mental or even a minor action that through repetition reaches the threshold of violence. Violence is any highly energetic form of relating to a person, including oneself, that is jarring, turbulent, and distorting. Can you identify any time in the last few days when you treated yourself in a discordant, abrupt, or distorting manner?

It may be hard for you to accept that some of your daily thoughts and actions are actually self-harming, but if someone were hitting you in your stomach, squeezing your neck, or not letting you breathe, you'd quickly label such behavior as violent. Yet when these same painful sensory experiences arise in reaction to your own thoughts or actions, you may fail to see them as violent. In your daily life, have you not repeatedly experienced these bodily sensations or others like them?

The Trappist monk and spiritual author Thomas Merton once said, "To allow oneself to be carried away by a multitude of conflicting concerns, to surrender to too many demands, to commit to too many projects, to want to help everyone in everything is itself to succumb to the violence of our times." Obviously Merton wasn't speaking about pathologically self-destructive behavior. Instead he was drawing our attention to the shadow side of normative, even seemingly positive, culturally approved behavior. He was referring to how we do great violence to ourselves simply by the manner in which we go about arranging our lives.

The Roots of Violence against Oneself

Most people perpetrate this violence against themselves by mistakenly identifying with various thoughts that arise due to impersonal conditions. The body and mind's well-being are the innocent victims. Each individual has a unique pattern of self-violence that results in their life being more full of emotional or physical harm than it need be. For example, if you identify yourself as someone who gets things done, you may inflict self-violence through over-scheduling yourself and taking on excess responsibility. This *addiction to busyness* is a common form of self-violence in Western culture. Three primary reasons for an addiction to busyness are wanting to avoid difficult emotions or situations, needing to feel important, and avoiding the feeling that your life is meaningless. A compulsion to over-schedule also sometimes comes from endless wanting, or a fear of not being good enough, or from being disorganized and undisciplined.

Practicing Nonviolence

Whenever I give a talk on violence against oneself, almost everyone squirms. No one wants to hear it. I will ask the question, "Are you, in an obvious manner or in a series of subtle, covert actions, being violent with yourself?" Usually people want to assure me that while they may work too hard at times, stay in an unhealthy relationship, eat too much, or sleep too little, they would not characterize their behavior as violent toward themselves. Yet once they've closely examined their lives, person after person experiences a moment of self-recognition that at first can be painful and embarrassing.

Failure to recognize violence against oneself is one of the great denials of our time. People are very willing to talk about the violence that the world does to them, but they're much less willing to own the violence that they do to themselves. Violence against oneself can most easily be recognized in the experience of the body in daily life. You already know the general health problems that come about because of stress, sleep deprivation, and constant strain. You may not identify them as examples of violence to yourself, but anytime you make your-self sick or dysfunctional it is an act of violence for which you need to take responsibility. We all know people who are overworked or have too much stress, which causes problems with their digestive system, heart, or other parts of the body, but who never see their behavior as being self-violent.

Similarly, you are being violent toward yourself if you engage in self-criticism or self-demeaning language; or if you use alcohol or drugs or eat excessively when you are restless, sad, or angry; or if you neglect your physical or emotional needs or deny your enthusiasms. Such behavior cannot be rationalized by claims of indifference or negative thoughts toward yourself.

Of course you may well want something in your life so much that you are willing to take the chance of hurting your body by driving it too hard. But usually a conscious, short-term exertion to reach a goal is not what causes violence to oneself. More often it is a matter of long-term disregard of the signals of imbalance. This disregard comes from repeatedly getting so caught in wanting or fearful mind states that you're unable to reflect on your own behavior. You may have a surface-level awareness of the distress you are feeling in your body, but you don't sincerely respond to the discomfort. In such instances you are in a driven state, controlled by your mind's imaginary creations rather than your inner values.

It's often hard to make the distinction between the mind states of fear and wanting and your inner values because there is such a strong tendency to identify with these mind states. But if you observe yourself closely, you will see that an endless number of mind states arise each day, independent of any intention on your part. The way to freedom from self-violence is to separate from these thoughts by getting to know your mind. This is the underlying purpose of mindfulness.

Taking Time Out

As the Thomas Merton quote points out, if you abuse your time, you are participating in violence against yourself. This may be in the form of over-scheduling to the point that you rob yourself of the experience of being alive. Or it may be in the form of allocating your time in a manner that doesn't reflect your priorities. Both create a distortion or infringement of self through strain and turbulence. When you treat your time as though you are a machine—a doing machine—you are committing violence against the sacredness of life itself.

Another abuse of time that disturbs your well-being occurs if you succumb to the modern-day compulsion to avoid boredom at all costs. In our stimulation-based culture, there is near hysteria in the compulsion to constantly seek fulfillment through activity, which leaves no time for the quietness of simply being present with yourself. Do you allow yourself time each day, or even weekly, to exist without an external purpose and without even background music or television? Empty time is vital to your well-being, and to deny yourself this nourishment is an act of violence.

You may ask why you continue to abuse your time and your body when you have the option to live more peacefully. Or you may say that you feel as though you have no choice but to be harsh toward yourself because your life situation is such a struggle. Under either circumstance you push the body and strain the mind violently because you are filled with the tension that comes with the feeling that there's not enough of something in your life, whether it's money, love, adventure, or confidence.

Feelings of inadequacy, vulnerability, longing, or not having enough are an inevitable part of the human experience. You cannot stop them from arising, but you can stop such feelings from controlling your life by changing how you perceive them. If you refuse to identify with these feelings, disown them as being neither you nor yours, thus seeing them simply as emotional states of mind that come and go, you will discover there is the possibility for some inner harmony even under difficult circumstances.

For instance, let's assume you can't change your work schedule, and it seems so overwhelming to you that you regularly get very tense and anxious about it. You can experience the schedule as much less violent by not thinking about it in its entirety except when you're in planning mode. The rest of the time you just do what the plan calls for, concentrating on the task in front of you without adding the thought, "Here I am with all this work and so much more to do this week."

Another method you can use to cope with over-scheduling is to notice each time you experience fear or wanting while thinking about all you have to do. Consciously label these feelings as fear and wanting in your mind and then see for yourself that they originate as impersonal mind states, the way a storm forms due to weather conditions. The land that receives the storm does not own it, and the storm is certainly not the land; it's just a storm, which because of its own characteristics can cause damage. So it is with the stormy situations in your life. There is a tendency to both deny and take ownership of fear or wanting. This misconception leads you to believe you should be able to control them, which in turn causes the physical contractions and mental anguish that constitute violence to oneself.

You Have No Right to Self-Violence

Inner development and maturity come from acknowledging to yourself that you are being violent with a human being; the fact that you happen to be the human being who is being hurt does not change the truth of the violence. From a moral perspective, it's never right to hurt any human being, including yourself, for selfish reasons or because of sloppy attention to the consequences of your actions. Understanding this is your first step in practicing nonviolence toward yourself.

One Life Balance client, Adrian, who suffers from self-loathing, is a prime example of someone who justified mistreating herself for many years. When she described her life during our first session, I was pained to hear how filled it was with self-violence—she isolated herself from others without acknowledging she was doing so, and she didn't make room in her life for activities that would bring personal growth and enjoyment. In Adrian's second session, when I had her map out her entire life on a whiteboard, the exercise revealed to her how little care she gave herself. Her one positive activity was shopping. She enjoyed doing it and had excellent taste. But in almost every other aspect of her life she neglected or overrode her needs. Work was the center of her life, but she was exhausting herself by making her job more stressful than it needed to be. She felt something was wrong, and although she had been seeing a psychiatrist, she remained frozen in her pattern of self-violence.

Over a two-year period, Adrian has transformed in many ways. She now volunteers for a cause she cares deeply about and that involves meeting a lot of people, she's fulfilling a lifelong dream of studying the piano, she's learned to meditate and do yoga, and she's changed her diet and her job! So, does this mean Adrian has fixed herself? Not totally. Her pattern of self-violence, which started in relationship to her family, still shows up in how she disregards her body, the negative terms in which she talks about herself, and how she denies herself friendship.

For Adrian shopping is truly a form of creative expression, a talent others who lack the skills or interest would benefit from, but she hasn't found a way to make this gift work as a career. It may be the same for you—your career may not provide you with an outlet to express yourself. Denial of self-expression is another form of violence against oneself. A Life Balance client who is an accountant solved this problem by starting a sideline career as a bodyworker; another returned in midlife to playing in a band. If you hear yourself saying, "I have no choices," beware that it could be a signal that you are being violent to yourself.

Stopping the Violence

You learn to stop being violent to yourself in steps. The first step is to be mindful of the harm your inner criticism, busyness, and self-abuse do to you. Just because it is you who are being mistreated doesn't permit you to justify creating such suffering. The second step is to see that in harming yourself, you cause distress to others, particularly those close to you. Causing harm to others through violence toward yourself is also unacceptable. It is irresponsible and self-centered. The third step is cultivating compassion and self-acceptance for you just as you are. If you could magically be a better version of yourself, you already would be. The fourth step is to notice the sincerity of your heart and all your other admirable traits. You have innate worth that is independent of all the desires of your wanting mind. To stop being violent toward yourself, it isn't necessary to love yourself, but you must at least view yourself as worthy of care.

Next you begin to examine why you are so driven, restless, angry, or defeated that you are caught in a pattern of self-violence. Notice how your mind has a tendency to think it needs something—it wants more of what you already have, or wants what you do not have, or wants to be rid of something. You will discover that your wanting mind is often the cause of the busyness, the over-scheduling, the over-indulgence, and the self-neglect.

Observe how your mind can be a little dictator, sitting on a throne, arms crossed, pouting and demanding that things you like should stay the way they are forever and what you do not like should disappear immediately. This craving to hold on to what you like and to get rid of what you find difficult is both the source of suffering in life and the origin of violence against oneself. By practicing living with things as they are, you will discover that while life may not be less painful, your experience of it is immeasurably better. Also, fully accepting what is true in the moment is the only firm place to begin to make changes in your life. Living in the moment is not a onetime commitment but something that has to be done again and again, indeed in every moment.

Nonviolence to oneself is a lifelong practice in which there are ever more subtle levels to discover. The more you are able to be with yourself in a nonviolent way, the less harm you will do to another. Be gentle with the body and mind and refuse to get caught in believing that for you to be happy things have to be a certain way.

Are You Being Self-Violent?

It's not always easy to recognize when you're being self-violent. Therefore it can be helpful to do an assessment of your overall life balance. If this assessment indicates major imbalance, then you are being violent against yourself. For each of the following statements, indicate the degree that it is true for you on a scale of 1–10, with 10 being most true.

1. I have enough energy to accomplish everything I need to do or want to do in my daily life.

2. I have enough time to accomplish everything I need to do or want to do in daily life.

3. I am satisfied with my life.

4. I can manage the amount of pressure I feel in my life.

5. I don't feel as though I have excessive stress. (In my Life Balance work, I make a distinction between pressure and stress: pressure is the size of the responsibility you're carrying and it can lead to strain; stress is your nervous system's reaction to pressure, and it creates anxiety.)

6. I don't feel anxious or worried about my life.

7. I don't have a major change or transition happening in my life right now.

8. I have a good support system to help me deal with pressure.

9. I'm doing a good job of taking care of my body.

10. I get sufficient sleep.

11. I eat a healthy diet.

12.   I have no major health issues at present.

13.   I wake up in the morning feeling enthusiastic about the day.

14.   I create rest and recovery periods in my life.

15.   I have fun and laughter in my life.

16.   I feel as though I am growing in wisdom.

17.   I feel as though my heart is open.

18.   I feel good about myself.

19.   I have good friends that I spend sufficient time with.

20.   I feel as though my life has a direction.

Total your score. If it's less than 100, it's urgent that you take corrective action. If it's between 100 and 149, you still need to attend to the imbalance, although not as urgently. If your score is 150 or above, your life is relatively balanced, but you want to continually be working to improve your score.

Chapter 17

Practicing Self-Restraint

You have within you an instinctive drive to immerse yourself in life, to partake of its offerings. The need for personal power and to make your mark in the world, the desire to be creative, and the wish for recognition are all manifestations of this instinctive drive. This drive and the mental and physical energy that you put into it are forces you must learn to balance. When they are in balance, these forces provide vital energy for engaging in life and form the basis for a healthy ego. When they are off-kilter, you may experience ambivalence, ambiguity, depression, or emotional chaos.

You also have within you an instinct toward self-restraint, an inclination to participate in something greater than fulfilling your ego's desires, which counterbalances the endless cycle of wanting one thing after another. Think of it as an intuitive urge to be free of your ego-centered striving. This instinct is one reason why being a parent is so rewarding for many people: the selflessness that comes from unconditional love provides more meaning and purpose in life than trying to satisfy ego desires. It is also why people enjoy serving those in need. This instinct toward restraint has the same goal as your drive to immerse yourself in life: to find happiness.

Self-restraint is recognized in most religious traditions as a vital step toward finding a center of being other than the ego. It is most visible in monks and nuns who have renounced the life of a house-holder, forsaking sexual pleasure, marriage, family, and material pos-sessions to devote themselves to their inner development. We admire, even envy, these men and women for the simplicity and integrity of their lives, even though we are unable or unwilling to renounce the desire that keeps us constantly scrambling.

Of course renunciation is not the exclusive property of nuns and monks. But if you are living in the world, how do you approach life with exuberance while managing to avoid being enslaved by its false promises? You may ask, "Aren't I supposed to be happy? And aren't material and emotional rewards the basis of happiness?" The answer is more complicated than a simple yes.

You know from experience how endless the world of wants is. You desire creature comforts, emotional reinforcement, security, and the power to control yourself and your environment. This thirsting leads to emotional clinging. You come to believe your happiness and peace are dependent upon these desires being met, which never seems to happen. Monks and nuns use renunciation to free themselves from this cycle of misery. Renunciation practice simplifies life and creates spaciousness in the mind that allows for deep insights to arise. When desire arises for that which has been renounced, there is still a strug-gle, but the struggle is focused on working with the desire, not on how to get the desired object.

You may be thinking that you'll pass on any exploration of renunciation practice and skip to the next chapter. But first consider this: There are three renunciations you can practice, any one of which will dramatically change your life. None involves giving up your job, marriage, or sex life or even forsaking buying that new car you've been dreaming about. Yet if practiced diligently, these practices will bring you greater happiness and inner peace.

Surrender Self-Righteousness

The first of these renunciations is giving up your attachment to being right—right in your opinions, judgments, or interpretations. You know this inner experience of attachment to being right—you are all puffed up with judgment and rigid in your convictions. You may feel flushed or indignant, defensive, or martyred when others do not agree with you.

This practice means renouncing the need to be right in your interactions with those around you—your significant other, colleagues at work, even your children. It also means forsaking being right about your life story, which may involve having been wronged or not receiving proper care or recognition in the past. In this practice you release your clinging to that story even though you still feel it is true. Additionally, you renounce your attachment to being right about the future and monitor yourself for ways in which you set yourself up so you can later say to yourself or others, "I was right all along!"

In practicing this form of renunciation, you aren't supposed to abandon what you feel to be true or forgo seeking justice for what you know to be wrong—quite the opposite. You fully embrace your truth. You state it clearly, stand up for your values, and fight injustice in your own life or wherever you encounter it. It means simply that you cease to be attached to your truth. It is what you believe; therefore you live it, bearing in mind that there is no monopoly on truth. You acknowledge to yourself that God is not whispering in your ear and that there is no justification for sitting on a throne of righteousness where you either tolerate or condemn those who have a different truth.

An example of this from my own life is how I regard the death penalty. I am absolutely convinced that the death penalty is a terrible mistake. I find it morally indefensible to kill in the name of punishment. Many people who were previously sentenced to death have had their convictions overturned because of recent advances in DNA testing; therefore it seems obvious to me that the death penalty is unconscionable. Ironically, many of those sentenced to death were the victims of false identification, a prime example of someone believing they knew something to be true when it wasn't. It's easy for me to be judgmental about those who take a different view on this subject. Yet when I reflect, I see that my belief, no matter how supported by evidence it is, is only a view. It doesn't entitle me to feel self-righteous, and it is clearly wrong to condemn others when it is their view, not them, with which I have issue.

This same perspective applies to personal situations. You may have had an abusive or neglectful parent or been in a manipulative relationship in which the other person was dishonest. Even so, your feelings are still only a view, a way of responding to the situation; they are not absolute. You stand up for them because they are your truth. It is not only your right to do so; it is your obligation. But you do so without attachment. If you discover that some of your perceptions are wrong, you're okay, because your self-esteem is not based on being right. Instead your worth comes from being someone who stands for your truth and remains open to new understanding.

The Dalai Lama provides a great example of not being attached to one's truth. When asked about the conflict between science and Buddhism, he replied, "If science proves a teaching of Buddhism wrong, then that teaching needs to change." In silent meditation retreats, students will sometimes have an unexpected realization about the dissolution of a marriage or relationship. They suddenly see that what they had believed to be true was really just their view of what happened, a view that didn't include all the factors contributing to the breakup. Each time this occurs, the student reports how freeing it is to stop dragging around their long-held complaint against the other person.

Stop Measuring Your Worth by Your Success in the World

The second renunciation is giving up measuring how successful your life is by how well your desires are met. Most people measure the success of their lives in just this manner: are they getting what they want in material objects, relationships, recognition, and personal health? It takes so little reflection to see that this is an unreliable manner for measuring the worth of your life. I am not saying you should give up your desires or forsake moving toward them. Desires—be they physical, emotional, or spiritual—are part of the ecology of your life. They are the flowering of the desert in the midst of the harsh conditions that surround all life.

Desires are useful for creating goals, for organizing your time. You can have skillful goals that keep you in a healthy balance and that change and mature with your life experience. It is just that you don't determine your self-worth by the success you have in reaching those goals. Instead you measure the success of your life by how well your actions reflect the intentions that are formed by your core values. To practice this renunciation requires that you trust that your life will turn out as best it can if you constantly act from your intentions, mindfully learning from whatever circumstances arise.

When I give talks on renunciation, I often get negative reactions to this one. One entrepreneur angrily stated that he had to measure life by how well his desires were met; after all, he had employees, stockholders, and creditors depending on him. I asked him if he really believed he controlled the success of his company and if market conditions, good fortune, the acts of his competitors, the creativity of those with whom he worked, his own creativity, or even his health were within his power. Of course he had to say no.

We are all subject to conditions beyond our control. This is an overwhelmingly reliable guideline for life choices, yet it is so hard to accept. In your role as a parent, leader, teacher, employee, care provider, or whatever, you cannot control outcomes, but you can be responsible for your intentions. You can put all your effort into fulfilling your responsibilities and reaching your goals, while being patient, persistent, and courageous—but that's it. To assume more is not only unrealistic; it is hubris. By focusing on your intentions, you align your attention with the area where your diligence can actually manifest. In making this shift, you also free yourself from your ego's demand to have things just as you want them.

Give Up Being the Star of Your Own Movie

The third renunciation is to give up being the star of your own movie. Without ever thinking about it, most people experience each arising moment from the point of view that it is happening to them. One of my teachers, Ajahn Amaro, illustrates this point by asking, "Have you ever noticed that when you get on the highway at rush hour it is everyone else who is the traffic, never you?" This feeling of being at the center of your experience, as if it is happening for and to you, leads you to make personal much of what is in fact impersonal. It causes you to make small things important that you later realize were not important. It adds tension to many moments of your daily life that is not inherently there.

Once while attending a three-month silent retreat, I had the realization that my story of having had a difficult father was strictly my view, which arose from being the star of my own movie. My father may or may not have regarded himself as a difficult father, but it certainly was not his primary means of identifying himself. His movie was not limited to his relationship to me; it was about his own difficult and emotionally challenged life, in which I was simply one part. This new perspective unburdened me and allowed me to cease identifying with being the son of a difficult father.

The same is true of your movie. You're definitely in it, and it is critical that you play your part as best you're able. Sometimes your part *is* to be the focus of your movie, either because you're dealing with some aspect of your development or you're involved in a group activity that requires it. But even then the movie is not really about you; you are an actor in a movie that is much larger and more mysterious than the narrative you tell yourself. And it involves a web of people, events, and conditions that started long before you were born.

When you cease being the star of your movie, you are far more able to fully participate in the movie yet not be consumed by it. This is illustrated beautifully in the ancient Hindu allegory the Bhagavad Gita, when Lord Krishna tells the warrior Arjuna that much of life is about simply fulfilling the duties and responsibilities of the part one is cast into by birth and past actions. This understanding, Krishna assures Arjuna, is critical to finding freedom, to liberating the mind from delusion. It is why cultivating your values and intentions matters so much. You never know what part you will be required to play under what circumstances, so there is nothing to rely on but your core values and living them as best you are able.

When You're No Longer the Star

Several therapists have reported to me that they have used the three renunciations with some patients with good results; however, one psychotherapist told me that while he thought the first two are excellent, I was mistaken about the third renunciation. "People need to become more of a star in their own movie, particularly people with low self-esteem," he said. He may be correct, but in my experience, if your self-esteem is contingent on seeing yourself as the center of all that happens to you, it can cause a great deal of agony.

It is especially hard to move beyond being the star of your movie if you have experienced a trauma in the past and you have created a self that is the star of the trauma. You cling to this identity despite how terrible it feels. I ask people on retreat who are struggling with traumatic memories, "If you are caught in a rainstorm and you get wet, does that make you rain?" Of course they say it doesn't. Then I say, "But you are wet nonetheless and you have to deal with being wet—towel off, put on dry clothes, etc. It is the same with trauma and hard times. They get you wet and you have to take care of yourself, but you are not the trauma."

When you start to realize that there is a "star" feeling in you, no matter how little you may think of yourself at times, new understanding becomes available. You realize that much of your anxiety about what might happen is self-induced pressure that comes from identifying with the perspective from which you are experiencing an event, like in the traffic example. You mistakenly believe you are somehow supposed to make everything turn out just right. The unfolding of life has no center, or, said another way, every point is equally the center. Either way there is no star; no one, including you, has to take all the pressure, to rise to the performance of a star. It is the unfolding of life itself that is at the heart of each moment. You only have to respond appropriately from your core values.

Each moment of life really weighs almost nothing, despite how heavy we often feel. The heaviness comes from our delusion, which causes us either to try to hold on to the moment, if it is pleasant, or to push it away, if it is unpleasant. Appearances to the contrary, we are not separate from other people or our environment. Every moment of experience is made up of interconnecting conditions, which, in that moment, are totally dependent on one another.

When you practice this renunciation, a feeling of spaciousness arises in your life. You may even experience a sense of ease in your life because you cease to be seduced by the mind's tendency to be reactive.

Touch the Sacred

You can practice each of these renunciations just as you are today. Some years ago I started with not being the star of my own movie. I could see that I was quite attached to being the star of my own movie. Yet I could also see that this brought stress, not happiness. So I began just as you would, with the recognition that practicing this renunciation is worth the effort. I understood that I was not giving up something that gave me happiness; rather I was letting go of something that as best I could determine was not serving me well at all.

Each of these practices is difficult. Sometimes you remember that you are doing the practice, but most of the time you completely forget. Then gradually you start to remember more often. One day you genuinely feel the relief that comes because, at least on that occasion, you actually did the practice. You start to see the subtle ways your mind creates holding, and you gain a felt sense of the need for some kind of renunciation. You begin to see the humor in your own mental gymnastics and how repetitious the mind is.

There comes a moment when you are really miserable from a sense of self-righteousness, or because you did not get what you wanted, or from feeling pressure as the star of your movie. It is not that different from other similar moments, yet this time you recognize that your suffering is not coming from your life but from how your mind is reacting. Then you get really interested in the practice because you know for yourself that it is a path to your happiness.

Renunciation Practice

1. Upon waking each morning for the next week, notice how many times your mind desires something. Try and keep an accurate count. The desire may be really small, like wanting to stretch, or moderate, like wanting a cup of coffee, or stronger, such as wanting a coworker to go along with your opinion in a meeting later in the day. What effect does this seemingly endless stream of desires have on your sense of well-being?

2. Now imagine yourself having only half that number of desires in a morning. What would your mind do with all that extra space? Almost everyone spends so much of their energy in wanting—wanting out of habit, not out of necessity. Start to notice the difference between necessity and habit in your wants.

3. Think of something in your life that would be helpful for you to give up but to which you're very attached. Notice your resistance. Observe how easily one part of your mind can see the rationale for renunciation while the other part wants what it wants. Now go through the same process with something that you're less attached to. You will find the resistance is still there but is not so daunting. Take this smaller renunciation on as a practice.

4. Notice that when you start thinking about renunciation how easy it is to get a case of the "shoulds." I should renounce eating fatty foods. I should renounce arguing with my difficult sibling. I should renounce staying up late. Renunciation doesn't arise from feeling that you should do something but rather from the heart being motivated by the good that will come of it.

Chapter 18

Overcoming Ordinary Compulsiveness

I have a friend who diligently phones each member of his family every week despite the fact that these conversations always upset him because of the way they disparage one another. Yet he doesn't wait for them to call him; week after week he makes the calls, and week after week he relives his family's drama. Another friend, who is very accomplished and has a luxurious lifestyle, has a habit of always steering our conversations around to talking about his various achievements and what a great life he has. His need for recognition is so strong he doesn't realize that it dominates and therefore limits our friendship. Both of my friends suffer from what I call *ordinary*, or *everyday*, *compulsion*—the irresistible drive or urge to repeatedly think, speak, or act in a manner that is unskillful and sometimes harmful.

Ordinary compulsion is a reactive state of mind that interferes with the natural flow and rhythm of your life. It can prevent you from acting from your deepest intentions and deprive you of genuine choices. Ordinary compulsion can interfere with getting things done or prevent you from letting go of a disappointment. It can cause you to get stuck in a sort of emotional eddy so that you're unable to move ahead in some aspect of your life. My friend who calls his family every week is caught in one of these eddies. When I suggested to him that he wait and see which family members called him, he responded that his sense of family duty wouldn't permit him to do that. Ordinary compulsion can also make it difficult for you to build strong friendships, as evidenced by my friend who is habitually self-referencing.

The cost of ordinary compulsion isn't always so obvious. For instance, you may know someone who won't delegate work and does everything herself. Outwardly it may appear that she has really high work standards; inwardly, though, she may be negatively motivated by a fear that she is only worth what she accomplishes and therefore is suffering from overwhelming performance anxiety.

The Importance of Acknowledging Compulsions

In my experience working with meditation students and Life Balance clients, I've observed that most people have some form of ordinary compulsion but aren't aware of it or the negative effect it has on their lives, and in some cases they may even deny the obvious harm they're causing. Thus, like the proverbial elephant in the room that nobody sees, ordinary compulsion is largely ignored; however, it signifies an underlying emotional imbalance that, once acknowledged, can be addressed.

Ordinary compulsion shows up in your life in subtle ways that can seem normal, which can make it difficult to discern. For instance, when you're talking to someone and there's a lull in the conversation, do you jump in and say something? Like my friend, do you go fishing for compliments? Or conversely, do you frequently compliment other people? Do you act differently around a particular person? All of these may seem like normal behaviors, but when you examine the underlying motives, you may realize that they're actually forms of ordinary compulsion. The urge to say something when there's a lull in conversation may mean that silence makes you feel insecure. Fishing for compliments may reflect a desperate need to feel validated, while handing out compliments to others may be a manipulative attempt to get them to like you. And you may act differently around a particular person because you're jealous of her or want her attention.

If ordinary compulsion often seems like normal behavior, then how can you recognize it? When a behavior is a *pre-scripted response to a recurring feeling of inner pressure*, then it is more than likely ordinary compulsion. Ordinary compulsion can be felt in the body as an overwhelming sense of pressure or urgency to act immediately in a certain way—for instance, the nervousness you might feel in the presence of your boss. You're not only compelled to relieve the inner pressure you're feeling, but your options for responding are limited to a narrow range of words and actions. So you blurt out words that you know will create trouble, or you volunteer to take on a responsibility when you know you shouldn't, or you give in to a demand just to relieve the tension, or you won't stop working on something even though you've already done more than what was expected, because you just can't let it go.

Let me be clear that I'm not referring to addiction or obsessive-compulsive disorder (OCD), as defined by *The Diagnostic and Statistical Manual of Mental Disorders*, which should be treated through psychotherapy. Nor am I talking about delusional jealousy or what's called the Othello syndrome, after the Shakespearean character whose obsessive belief that his wife had been unfaithful drove him to murder her even though he loved her. I'm definitely not talking about that kind of obsessive behavior, although sometimes ordinary compulsion can feel like that, especially in romantic relationships. Who hasn't ever suffered a broken heart and pined, "I can't live without him!" or her, as the case may be?

Ordinary Compulsion at Work and in Families

In addition to noticing that almost everyone displays ordinary compulsion in personal interactions, I've observed that it is prevalent in the workplace. For example, within many organizations there can be someone in a leadership position who compulsively takes credit for everything good that happens. Sometimes that credit is due because the person really is key to the organization's success; however, he could easily share the credit but is totally unable to do so. Then there is the leader who compulsively takes all the credit when in fact he didn't do anything to deserve it! Both of these types of compulsive behavior can be very demoralizing and disempowering for everyone else in the organization.

Ordinary compulsion exists among employees in an organization too. Oftentimes there is someone who compulsively competes with his coworkers and refuses to act as a team member, or someone who compulsively finds fault with the organization and gets people to side with her against the imaginary foe that she's always opposing. And there are people who gossip in order to make themselves seem more important within the organization than they actually are.

Ordinary compulsion is present within every family because each member's role is so well defined that it is almost impossible to view yourself as anything other than mom, dad, son, or daughter. But in dysfunctional families these ordinary compulsions become exaggerated or distorted, and when left unchecked, they create a continuing pattern of misery. One family member compulsively does or says something that injures another family member or that undermines the relationship between two other family members, which then causes them to react unskillfully. Then other family members compulsively rush to the defense of one or the other party. These compulsive behaviors feed on one another, causing a ripple of pain throughout the whole family.

The Consequences of Compulsive Behavior

All ordinary compulsions have consequences; they're not just temporary moments of discomfort that disappear. For instance, compulsive behavior in the workplace that isn't controlled by leadership can cause disharmony and emotional chaos that demoralizes staff and diminishes creativity, productivity, and accountability.

Some years ago I had a Life Balance client, Craig, who was considering whether he should switch careers even though he was quite successful in his field and was already in his late forties. He owned his company and liked his work but reported that he had begun to feel constant tension in his body. He had also developed a dislike for being in the office.

Craig had a charming personality and gave the appearance of self-control, so no one else noticed his tension, but it was alarming him. He couldn't understand where it was coming from. I found his situation puzzling too. I had Craig complete a questionnaire that I've developed to help pinpoint where imbalance is occurring in a person's life, but nothing showed up in his assessment. Finally, I had him describe in detail how his business worked, including how the profit, power, and glory were allocated.

He was quite generous in praising the contributions of others, but when I asked for specifics, Craig became defensive. And with good reason! He totally lacked largesse when it came to sharing the rewards that were the result of everyone's labors. He was generous in small ways, such as paying for dinner and giving employees extra time off, and to a certain degree he was good about sharing power. But he was stingy in his allocation of the glory and particularly tight-fisted with money, even with people who were his partners. As a result the company experienced constant turnover among employees and partners. I'm sure the reason he lost so many key people was because they felt exploited and unappreciated.

Craig acted in this harmful manner out of compulsion. He had a deeply rooted sense of his needs not ever being met, and therefore he could not be generous with others. On an unconscious level Craig knew he was acting unfairly and, therefore, had to override his own sense of fairness in order to rationalize his behavior. Craig was paying a heavy price for his compulsion, in the form of chronic tension that was wrecking his body. He also didn't have business associates that he could call friends, and his employees didn't trust him. It was no wonder he disliked being at the office.

Investigating Ordinary Compulsion

Thankfully, ordinary compulsion is susceptible to change. Through mindful investigation, it's possible to develop a genuine relationship with ordinary compulsion. You can then start to exercise choice in how you respond to the circumstances of your life, rather than react slavishly.

The process of investigation begins with noticing the components that make up ordinary compulsion. It helps to think of ordinary compulsion as an *unattended, habitual impulse.* By reflecting on the meaning of each of these words, you can gain valuable insight into the nature of compulsion.

Impulse is the original uncontrollable urge, which causes the inner pressure that leads you to say or do something reactive. Throughout the day you experience many naturally arising impulses that you have control over—to eat, rest, exercise, connect with friends, etc. However, the kind of impulse that leads to compulsion is a complex of thoughts, mental images, urges, and strong body sensations that shows up and acts on its own. This original impulse was created by conditions that were once present in your life but are no longer there. For instance, someone raised by parents who argued violently may compulsively avoid confrontation even when they need to speak up for themselves.

By *habitual* I mean that the impulse has developed independently of your core values, and it occurs over and over again when the causative conditions arise. It just happens, and as a result you never learn to recognize it or change: you compulsively speak when there's a lull in conversation, or get drunk in certain situations, etc. If you don't yield to the habitual impulse, you experience discomfort, disorientation, or anxiety. Sometimes when you give into a habitual harmful compulsion, you experience a temporary feeling of release, maybe even happiness. But usually you become disappointed with yourself and see that it's having an unwholesome effect.

By *unattended* I mean you haven't opened to investigating your habitual impulse. You don't yet see how it arises in reaction to causes and conditions that are impersonal despite the fact that they are happening to you. And you haven't fully accepted responsibility for any harm that your compulsion may be causing you or others. If you don't attend to it, your compulsion will persist and may even get worse.

One meditation student who was recovering from heart surgery compulsively ate large amounts of ice cream every night even though he knew it was potentially harmful. He was mystified by his behavior. As long as he identified with the urge, saw it as him or his, it was impossible for him refrain from acting it out. It took a while for him to realize that his compulsion was an independent complex, one that he needed to manage so he could say no to the overwhelming urge to eat ice cream when it arose.

Bringing Mindfulness to Bear on
Ordinary Compulsion

Ordinary compulsions are simply habitual impulses that you can free yourself from by repeatedly bringing mindfulness to the moment the impulse arises, or while you're in the midst of acting out your compulsion, or once it's passed. With mindfulness you'll begin to sense the original impulse as it is forming. You will feel it as tension in your body. If you can fully experience the felt sense of the impulse in your body, it will help anchor you in the moment and allow you to mindfully investigate it.

The more you practice being mindful of your habitual impulses, the better you'll get at recognizing them as they form and the causative conditions, which increases your chances of responding skillfully. For instance, you might be talking to your sibling on the phone when you notice a feeling of one-upmanship arising in you. You then realize that this impulse is rooted in a childhood pattern of sibling rivalry. Just noticing this gives you the freedom to relate differently to your sibling.

As you continue your investigation, you want to do so with compassionate curiosity, not with an attitude of "there's something wrong with me." Meeting ordinary compulsion with compassionate curiosity allows you to see the impersonal nature of it and that you have choice in how you respond. Initially your response may simply be awareness of the compulsion and the harm it's causing. But this already represents a significant shift. Then, as you stay mindful of the compulsion, you will start to develop a wider range of choices. One day you will realize that it's truly possible not to give in to the compulsion; from that moment on, you will have much more confidence in your ability to work with the compulsion.

If you want to deepen your investigation of ordinary compulsion, you might also recruit a friend to be a witness to a particular compulsion. For instance, if you're a workaholic but you really don't need to work as much as you do, you might ask your friend to ask, "Are you being compulsive?" when he sees that you're overworking. You're not asking your friend to fix you, just to be there for you. Alternatively, you might try this approach with a therapist.

In working with a particular compulsion, you might also try adopting behaviors that create a pause and give you time to understand your choices. For instance, if you're the one who always volunteers for extra office duties and ends up stressed, try one of these strategies the next time you're in a staff meeting and your boss asks for someone to take on more work: keep your mouth shut, excuse yourself to go to the bathroom, or volunteer someone else for the job! I'm only half joking, because someone who compulsively takes on extra work has a difficult time seeing that they have claimed the role of martyr. Others think you want to do more, so they're happy to let you! When you substitute one of the behaviors I've suggested, you signal to everyone that you're giving up being the martyr.

The Felt Sense of Letting Go of Compulsions

When you're no longer defined by your compulsions, you become open to subsequent realizations that can yield new understandings about what it means to have a heart and mind that are free. In the poem "Burnt Norton," from *Four Quartets*, T. S. Eliot eloquently captures this psychological and spiritual transformation that arises when you truly gain freedom from compulsion when he writes:

> *The release from action and suffering, release from the inner*
> *And the outer compulsion, . . .*

The "outer compulsion" that Eliot is pointing to is the kind that takes away your choice in interacting with the world, and the inner compulsion is the sort that imprisons you within yourself. As these compulsions are released, the possibility of living life with grace and joy is revealed. This sounds like a lofty aspiration, and indeed it is; nevertheless it is realized by humbly attending to your mundane, everyday compulsions.

Recognizing Compulsive Selfing

One category of ordinary compulsion that many people suffer from is what I call *selfing*; that is, obsessing about your own needs. Each of us exhibits some degree of selfing. A certain amount is healthy and necessary for negotiating your way in the world, but many people are *compulsively selfing*.

There are three ways in which selfing can manifest: selfishness, self-centeredness, and self-referencing. All three are the result of some degree of trauma or lack of emotional development. Reflect on the following questions to assess whether you have a tendency toward selfing. As you do this, notice that you may be selfing in one aspect of your life but not another. For instance, you may not self-reference with your children but do so compulsively when you interact with your spouse. Or you may not be selfing in your family life but you do it at work.

Once you become familiar with the three forms of selfing, you will begin to notice it in others as well. For example, you may be having difficulty in your relationship with a friend that stems from their selfing compulsion. Once you realize this, you can adjust your behavior and expectations to cope with their compulsion.

Selfishness

This is the most extreme form of selfing. It means that you focus on your own concerns excessively or exclusively and that you have a habit of seeking advantage at the expense and in disregard of others. It is often associated with a deep emotional wound.

No matter how much you have (wealth, material possessions, recognition, etc.), do you often feel as though you don't have enough?

Do you have a sense of entitlement that stems from bitterness or anger about something that happened to you?

Do you tend to be generous only when it serves your own purpose?

In conversation, do you have a habit of focusing mostly on what's relevant to you and have very little interest in listening to others?

Do you believe that others exist to satisfy your needs?

In a transaction or exchange, do you believe you are supposed to take as much as you can without considering what seems fair or what others need?

Do you frequently lack empathy for other people's struggles?

Do you often have a nihilistic or cynical view of the world?

Self-Centeredness

This form of selfing is not as extremely obsessive as selfishness, but it means that you're still excessively concerned with your own welfare.

Are you generous only when you think you'll be recognized or rewarded for it?

In conversation, do you only listen when you want some information or when you want to affect the other person in some way?

Do you compulsively interrupt others during conversations?

Do you have a habit of inconveniencing other people to get what you want or need?

In a transaction or exchange, do you take more than your fair share? Do you need to feel that you've gotten more than the other person?

Do you tend to assume that your opinions and beliefs are right?

Are you often the person who's at the center of any conversation?

Do you have a pattern of getting others to organize their lives around meeting your wants and needs?

Self-Referencing

In this form of selfing, you are not excessively concerned with your own welfare, but you compulsively compare yourself with others. Your perception of the world is narrow but not as extreme as the selfish or self-centered in dividual.

Are you always asking, "How does this affect me?"

When you are generous is it only within your frame of reference?

In conversation, do you listen from a comparing state of mind? Do you frequently respond to what the other person is saying by referencing yourself?

Is it hard for you to praise others or celebrate their success?

Do you have a continual need for recognition?

When you're not doing well, do you feel the need for a lot of sympathy?

Are you aware of other people's needs but you seldom put them ahead of your own?

Are you "at your best" only when you're with family or people you are identified with?

Are you seduced by praise? Do you become unsure of yourself or anxious if you don't receive positive feedback?

Chapter 19

Living Skillfully with the Difficult

As much as we would all prefer that it wasn't so, difficult times are an unavoidable part of the ever-changing stream of life. Difficulties come on their own accord irrespective of whether they are deserved or fair and regardless of our ability to bear them. The difficult can manifest in any aspect of life, including physical, mental, or emotional health; career or job; financial situation; and relationships with friends, family, and intimate partners. Sometimes the difficulties we encounter are minor and tedious but numerous. For example, you might have a difficult relationship with a sibling who constantly criticizes you; although no single instance of their judgment constitutes a significant hardship, you have an abiding sense of being treated unfairly. Sometimes difficulties are major and dramatic, such as the unexpected death of a loved one or losing your job. And sometimes you're faced with a difficulty that is constant and cannot be changed, such as a physical disability or chronic illness. It's essential that you learn to live skillfully with the difficult; otherwise you may collapse into destructive, negligent, or self-defeating behavior, which will only compound your suffering.

I use the phrase "learn to live skillfully with the difficult" because it points to the fundamental truth that *each of us has the capacity to accept, accommodate, and adjust to what cannot be changed.* The process of learning to live skillfully with the difficult is gradual and not easily or happily accomplished, but once learning has occurred you will discover that even in the midst of extreme difficulty, when the quality of your outer life may be greatly diminished, you still have an inner experience of well-being.

How Do You React to the Difficult?

If you want to change the way you respond to the difficulties in your life, it is first necessary to assess how your mind habitually reacts to the difficult and how your mind's reaction is reflected in your nervous system. Ask yourself the following questions about how you respond when difficulty arises:

- Does your mind become rigid or have a hard, relentless edge to it?
- Do you space out or resort to some other avoidance behavior in order to escape?
- Does your nervous system become tense?
- Does your mind become jumpy?
- Do you feel numb?
- Do you feel apathetic?
- Do you feel vulnerable?

These are all typical reactions that are not only unhelpful but actually make the difficult more difficult! They multiply the chaos in your life and interfere with your ability to clearly see your options for responding to the difficulty. You have these reactions because the difficulty can be threatening to your ego or even traumatizing; therefore your autonomic nervous system goes into fight-or-flight mode. You may become agitated, irritated, bitter, or angry or else collapse into helplessness, self-blame, disassociation, or self-pity.

Additionally, your mind may engage in various nonproductive attempts to change what can't be changed; it may push at the difficulty to get it to go away, or it may pull away in order to remove itself from the difficulty. Either way, the result is the same: your mind is in a constant state of tension. While it's certainly fine to want to minimize difficulty, it is counterproductive for your mind to be always pushing or pulling. Yes, it's terrible that you suffered a big financial loss or that you severely injured yourself, but the actual event has passed; therefore trying to change the reality of it because it's unpleasant is foolhardy and ultimately harmful to you. The unrelenting tension exhausts your nervous system and limits your mind's flexibility in responding to difficulties. Living skillfully with the difficult means that you no longer suffer these adverse side effects. Yes, you still must cope with difficulties, but your suffering isn't magnified by your reaction.

Relaxing Your Attention and Softening into Your Experience

The untrained mind naturally reacts unskillfully to difficulties because it does not realize that there is an alternative response, which is to *soften into the experience.* By this I mean that you can learn to relax your attention and cease to resist the unpleasant feelings that arise in response to difficult situations.

Attention is the capacity of your mind to focus where you direct it, and the *quality* of your attention can vary dramatically depending on your life circumstances. During difficult times, when it is disturbed by tension, your attention may have a jumpy, rigid, fixed, or fuzzy quality. As a result you may be unable to effectively respond to difficult circumstances. Therefore it's crucial to cultivate *relaxed attention.*

In relaxed attention your focus is neutral. There's no tension in your attention, so you feel more at ease in the face of difficulty. You cultivate relaxed attention by practicing noticing the tension underlying your attention whenever you experience something difficult and remembering your intention to relax your attention. Most of the time the tension will release immediately. If you are deeply enmeshed in a difficulty, it may take some time for this release to happen, but with continued practice you will develop the ability to focus on any degree of difficulty without added tension.

Relaxed attention sets the stage for softening into your experience. I like to use the phrase *softening into your experience* because it captures the felt sense of relief that occurs when you become mindful of your resistance to the difficult and then release it. Softening into your experience isn't about collapsing or quitting on yourself but rather about fully accepting that difficulty is a natural part of life. When you stop objecting to the difficult, two benefits arise: you suffer less, and you have more energy at your disposal to skillfully deal with the difficult when it arises.

Although you can practice softening into your experience anytime, the ideal time to begin is while meditating or doing contemplative prayer or when you're having a mildly pleasant experience. For example, if you're enjoying a beautiful sunset or a quiet moment, simply invite this softening into your experience. After practicing with the pleasant for several days or weeks, begin trying to soften into mildly unpleasant experiences, such as when you're waiting for someone who's running late or when you're arguing with your spouse. Pause for a moment, focus your attention on the feeling of this temporary difficult mind state, and then say to yourself, "I accept that this mind state is part of life." Notice if your mind stops resisting the difficulty, and if so, what happens next. Does your mind feel more spacious? Do you have more choices in how you respond to the difficulty? Do you feel that you're no longer defined by the difficulty? Don't expect the difficult to disappear from your life, but your relationship to it will undoubtedly change because your well-being won't be contingent on circumstances being different.

One Man's Journey to Softening into the Difficult

Jim is a Life Balance client who separated from his wife three years ago, after being married for several decades. The primary reason for the separation was that his wife is an alcoholic. After trying everything he could imagine to help her overcome her addiction, Jim finally decided to leave the marriage for the sake of his own survival. It was a very hard decision for him, and he continues to support his ex-wife in numerous ways.

Since the separation, Jim has been consumed by feelings of helplessness and survivor's guilt and has wrestled with the question of whether he was an enabler in his ex-wife's addiction. For more than a year after leaving the marriage, he lived in a barren apartment while his ex-wife lived in their beautifully decorated home, because he did not feel he had the right to create his own place as long as she was still struggling with her problems. As we've worked together, Jim has come to realize just how traumatizing it has been for him to watch the slow, steady deterioration of this woman he deeply cares for.

I had Jim explore softening into his experience and accepting that he could not control the situation. He now sees how tense his mind becomes each time he focuses on his ex-wife and has learned to relax his attention whenever he speaks to her or does something for her. Moreover, he sees how rigid his mind had become and how that rigidity was preventing him from moving on and creating a life for himself. In the process he also realized that he was angry and he behaved defensively toward her, which caused huge amounts of tension, and that his fear for her combined with his sense of helplessness had hardened him in a way that was causing him to dis-associate from life.

The change in Jim has been remarkable. It hasn't happened quickly or easily, but he has definitely developed a more easeful, open-hearted relationship to his ex-wife's difficulty. He remains very sad about her situation, but he is no longer caught in a reactive mind state in his relationship to it.

You Are Not Your Difficulty

Like Jim, you too may be forced to live with a difficult situation and may be unconsciously identifying with the limitations it creates and living out your role as a person with that difficulty. For instance, maybe you have a physical or mental condition that is chronic, such as Lyme disease or ADHD, or maybe you're a cancer survivor. It's easy to define yourself in terms of these conditions because it takes so much of your time and energy to deal with the difficulty, to begin to believe that "I'm a person with Lyme disease," or "I'm a person with ADHD," or "I'm a person with cancer."

If you find yourself anticipating how your difficulty will limit you in a situation or using it as an excuse to not show up, or if at every opportunity you tell friends or new acquaintances about your diffi-culty, then you have identified yourself with it. You are literally addicted to your difficulty. You are separating from life and denying yourself the possibility of unknown and unexpected joy by placing such distinct limits on who you can be.

You are not your difficulty; it is only one of the many things that characterize you. All your other characteristics—your generosity, friendliness, kindness, curiosity, willingness to learn, humor, loyalty, etc.—define you more accurately than whatever difficulty you may have in your life, no matter how great that difficulty is.

Skillful Means for Moving Beyond the Difficult

Once you've learned how to soften into your experience, you can begin to shift the way difficulties affect your body and your emotions and start to reframe the way you describe your situation to yourself and others. I once again recommend starting with awareness of the body; every strong emotion manifests in the body, so you can often recognize it as a physical sensation first. Moreover, when dealing with difficulties, you may harm your body in various ways: from the tension in your attention or the stress of your uncertainty, or from losing sleep or abusing food, alcohol, or drugs, etc. Softening into your experience allows you to realize the damage you are causing to your body and to take responsibility for nourishing it as best you're able during difficult times.

Likewise, softening into your experience allows you to become mindful of your emotions and to see how they are triggered by difficulties in your life. Notice how you relate to each of these emotions. Do you feed the emotion? Are you ashamed of it or do you deny its existence? Are you so identified with your difficult emotion that it is distorting the truth of your situation? Are you so overwhelmed by emotion that you are locked in an endless cycle of despair? Observe these emotions with great compassion and sympathy, for it's hard to cope with what's difficult in your life. It's very important that you be truthful with yourself about the emotions that arise in you in reaction to difficulties and not to judge yourself for having them. As with the body, do what you can to comfort the emotions, give yourself mental breaks, and find support from others.

Whatever emotions you are having, repeatedly remind yourself that they are just emotions, which arise and pass, and that they are simply the result of impersonal causes and conditions outside you. As you cease to be identified with these emotions, your mind will come back into balance.

Once you've regained a level of balance in body and emotion, you can start to reframe the way you describe your difficult situation to yourself and others. You may discover that your language is embedded with self-criticism, hopelessness, or self-pity, which not only makes you feel worse but also alienates and isolates you from others. Likewise, the narrative and prognosis you've internalized, the story you've identified with, may ignore what is good in your life.

Set an intention to practice being open to living with the difficult. You might say to yourself, "I'm going to make a practice out of living with difficulty. It is my value to meet difficulty and to interact with it as deeply as I can." By simply doing this, you already start to shift your orientation—the difficulty is no longer something that's separate from your life because you're no longer objecting to life being difficult sometimes. You're avowing your willingness to interact with and respond to what's difficult and to find meaning in it, even if the difficulty is something that's going to come again and again.

A few words of caution: If you're living with a difficult situation and find yourself in this moment at peace with it, don't go looking for the "ouch." It's unskillful to think, "I'm in a difficult situation, and therefore I'm supposed to feel how difficult my life is right now." When you do start feeling weighed down by the difficulty, repeat loving-kindness and compassion phrases, such as, "May I have a calm, clear mind in this difficult moment."

Another skillful means of building your capacity for living with the difficult is seeking support. That support may come from friends or family or a pet or being in nature. It might also be professional support, from a psychotherapist, perhaps, or a spiritual community. Sometimes you simply need to feel the presence of another person, or to know that someone cares about you, or to sense the beauty of the world. At other times you may need professional guidance to make your way through a difficulty. It isn't weak to seek help; it's an act of courage. You aren't being a burden to others by asking for help, as long as you respect their time and needs; instead you're giving them an opportunity to make a difference in the life of another.

Protecting Your Heart from the Difficult

One of the great challenges in life is to not allow the presence of the difficult in your life to shut down your heart. The Buddha taught that awareness of certain universal truths can prepare your heart for living with the difficult. The first of these truths is that everyone experiences difficulty, not just you or the people you care about. The second is that life is always changing, and there's no way you can ever get it to be just right. The conditions of your life—your financial situation, health, relationships, etc.—will change, and so will everyone else's; therefore you are having a shared experience in this perilous journey we call life.

Ultimately you are faced with this question: are you willing to accept life on its own terms? I have a friend who was riding his bicycle one evening when he lost consciousness because of an undiagnosed medical condition. When he awoke, he was lying on the ground and quadriplegic. He was in the prime of his life, an athlete, and he had done nothing careless, but he was suddenly faced with a dramatically life-altering difficulty.

It would have been so easy for my friend to quit, to become bitter about life, and to feel sorry for himself. Instead he accepted life on its terms. As he lay in the hospital, not knowing whether he would ever recover from his spinal injuries, he simply started trying to move some part of his body. Day after day he practiced moving something until finally one day he was able to flex the thumb on his right hand. It was several more days before he could move his other thumb and many more days before he could move the rest of his fingers and many weeks before he could move his arms. Months passed and he regained his ability to move his whole body, although in a limited manner.

My friend's recovery is an inspiring story; however, his life and the lives of his family are now dramatically different than before the accident. His life is simply *like this*. Living with the difficult is just one factor in his life among many, including his knowledge, his strong work ethic, and his love for his wife and daughter. Just as my friend continues to embrace his life with these new, difficult conditions, you too are challenged to find the beauty, joy, and meaning in the life you have.

Overcoming Personal Defeat

One kind of difficulty that can be particularly challenging is what I call *personal defeat*. A personal defeat occurs when you believe you have the capacity to achieve something that's really important to you but are unable to bring about the outcome you imagined. Instead of learning from your failure and moving on, you internalize it. If left unattended, a personal defeat can come to define how you view yourself and in turn limit your possibilities.

Can you recall a situation in your life where you experienced a failure and construed it to be a personal defeat? Maybe you tried to start your own business but were unsuccessful, or you didn't get accepted into the college of your choice, or your marriage ended in divorce. How did you handle this failure? Did you internalize it and begin to carry it around with you so that you relive the personal defeat over and over again?

An example of someone who suffered a personal defeat that she allowed to control her life is Pam, a Life Balance client. Soon after leaving graduate school, Pam was hired by a prestigious management-consulting firm and awarded an opportunity to manage a major project. Her colleagues who had been with the company much longer resented Pam for getting the management role, which they had not been offered, so they made her life hell. Because she was young and naive about office politics and lacked a protective mentor, Pam collapsed under the pressure and withdrew from the management position midway through the project. She stayed with the firm for several more years but never recovered from this defeat. When Pam came to see me, she was, a decade later, still agonizing over her failure, which had affected her career in unfortunate ways. She was afraid to take management jobs that were offered to her by other companies, she tended to take any negative feedback personally, and she would become defensive and angry if she felt disrespected by her peers. As a result she had not come close to living up to her potential.

In our work together, Pam came to realize that she remained traumatized by this personal defeat and that she had clung to it so strongly that it had become part of her identity. Moreover, she saw that her personal defeat had affected her romantic life; she had been involved in a series of long-term relationships with men she did not respect and whom she chose because she unconsciously felt they were all that she was worthy of.

Don't Be Defeated by Personal Defeat

As Pam's experience illustrates, a personal defeat can be so traumatizing that it becomes your frame of reference and defines how you see yourself. Conversely, you might simply not integrate the personal defeat into the context of your life and go on as though it never happened. Either way, it can haunt you for years. When a personal defeat doesn't get consciously integrated into your life, the memories, emotions, and body sensations associated with it can appear unexpectedly anytime and have a corrosive effect on your thought processes and decision making. For instance, right before coming to see me, Pam had interviewed for a management position with a high-profile company. She was excited about the job and had been told by the recruiter that it was hers "to lose." But during her final interview with the CEO, something in the conversation triggered her trauma, causing her to lose confidence, and she blew the opportunity.

The trauma of a personal defeat may characterize your life for many years, but it does not have to define it. *You do not have to be defeated by defeat.* Although you cannot change what happened, you can change how you relate to it. *If you fully accept personal defeat and embrace it as an inevitable part of life, then you can benefit from it.* By using the tools I've emphasized repeatedly throughout this book—mindfulness, intention, and compassion—it's possible for you to grow from your experience in such a way that your failure becomes an asset for the future. You will be transformed by the defeat into someone who is prepared to receive defeat when it comes again and has the capacity to consciously bear it.

Integrating Personal Defeat

You can move beyond personal defeat through a process of integration and redemption. As with other kinds of difficulty, you must first soften into your experience, which prepares you to acknowledge and accept your failure. Integrating personal defeat starts with reflecting on the original event without judging yourself or wanting the past to be other than it is. In your reflection you may feel deeply sorry that this personal defeat occurred. Why wouldn't you? If a friend or your child told you about a personal defeat they had experienced and were taking responsibility for, wouldn't you have sympathy for them, even if they were at fault? When you reflect on a personal defeat in this nonjudging, compassionate way, you may see what happened more clearly or differently. Or you may not. You may feel the personal defeat in a way that's kinder to yourself. Whatever unfolds is fine, because you're bringing up the personal defeat in a safe manner; therefore you can more fully accept it.

I once had a Life Balance client, Stewart, who experienced a devastating personal defeat as the leader of a high-profile company. To make matters worse, the story of his leadership failure became public and was published in several newspapers and magazines. Several months after his personal defeat, Stewart came to me desperately hoping to regain perspective. He had been lauded as an innovative leader for years, and now he was being dismissed as totally inept.

For our first few sessions together, I could not get Stewart to be present in his experience. He just kept repeating the story of his personal defeat over and over again, focusing each time on a different detail and trying to convince me why this or that news report wasn't true. The trouble, as I discovered during these first sessions, was that almost all the criticism was accurate. In order to move on, Stewart had to integrate the story of his defeat into his life. His challenge was to stay mindfully present to the feeling of his failure, no matter how unpleasant, and learn to be compassionate and patient with himself. It took almost a year for Stewart to accept that he had messed up, but eventually he was able to own his failure and regain his confidence in his abilities. He's now in the midst of starting up a new company and by all reports is doing far better.

Knowing the Four Kinds of Personal Defeat

In order to have a more empowered relationship to personal defeat, it helps if you can distinguish between the four different kinds of failure you may experience. Knowing the origins of your personal defeat will enable you to respond wisely.

1. *Failure in the external world.* You were unable to accomplish a worldly goal that was very important to you.
2. *Failure in your inner experience.* You disappointed yourself in some manner by not staying true to your values or by failing to live out your dreams the way you had hoped to.
3. *Failure in relationship with another person.* You alienated or failed to show up for a romantic partner, a friend, a coworker, or a family member.
4. *Failure in an organizational or group setting.* You compromised your standing in your workplace, your community, or even your family.

Worldly Defeat Feels like This

Worldly defeat comes from failing to accomplish something you set out to do, or from not being given the opportunity to try, or from not receiving the rewards or recognition you sought. For example, a Life Balance client, Adam, had tried to start up a company but failed. From his perspective, he blew his chance for success three times. When he set up the company, he failed to raise adequate capital because he wanted to keep a majority of the stock. Then he passed up a chance to sell the company at a good price, thinking he could get much more. And when he had to make a critical decision about which technology to use in his key product, he made a bad choice. Adam was devastated. He felt like he had not only let down his investors but had also let himself down. It was a personal defeat for him, and his failure as an entrepreneur became his story.

Adam generalized his failure and came to the conclusion that he lacks what it takes to be a leader. But during our work together, he realized that his problem wasn't that he was an ineffective leader; it was his greed, arrogance, and need to be seen as special that led to his downfall. He had failed to reign in his ego and succumbed to his greed. Adam came to see that his failure could incentivize him to let loose of needing to be special and to find humility. It was going to require a major effort on Adam's part because underneath his arrogance was a well of insecurity.

Failing Yourself Feels like This

The feeling of being disappointed in yourself comes from not being the person you wish you were. Maybe you let yourself down by doing something bad or were lazy, indulgent, or selfish. Perhaps you feel as though your life has no meaning, or you don't respect yourself, or you feel guilty or ashamed about what you've done with your life. For example, as Lee, a meditation student, neared retirement, he realized that although he had achieved some degree of professional success, he had always played it safe. He had never really stepped up to the plate, never had the experience of feeling that he was "going for it" just once in his career. Lee saw this as a major personal defeat and was convinced that it would haunt him the rest of his life.

You too may feel as though you never really stepped up to the plate. If you believe you're past the time in your life when "going for it" is possible, then I advise you to acknowledge to yourself that how you've lived your life up to this point has been disappointing and to fully surrender to the truth of it, without judging yourself for it. Simply acknowledge that "This is how my life is now," because in order to discover if change is possible, you have to start where you are. This may seem obvious, but oftentimes people don't want to face up to the truth of their situation, so they try to change while avoiding the uncomfortable feelings of what is true. You can still have a feeling of showing up 100 percent for life, even if the range of possibilities has dwindled.

Failure with Another Feels like This

Failure with another person can mean that maybe you failed to show up for a friend when they really needed you, or were unable to sustain a romantic relationship, or failed to stand up to someone's bullying, or took advantage of a close friend and lost their friendship. One of my meditation students, Kara, had always had a difficult relationship with her mother and was working on making peace with her. She wasn't hoping to reconcile with her mother, she just wanted to be able to be in her mother's presence without getting upset. But despite having made many attempts, Kara hadn't succeeded, and then her mother unexpectedly died. For Kara, this became a personal defeat that she carried around for years.

Failing within Your Organization Feels like This

This is the type of failure my client Pam experienced at her workplace. We are genetically hardwired to be part of a group—a family, tribe, or community. In fact the feeling of letting down your group or being rejected by the group distinguishes this type of defeat from failure in a relationship. You can feel a personal defeat in any group you are part of—your church or temple, your child's Parent-Teacher Organization, your workplace, the family you were born into, or the family you've made.

I've found that most people are good at recognizing this type of failure, but not so good at recovering from it. For example, a woman who attended one of my "Changes and Transitions" workshops told me that while growing up she never felt like she fit in with her family's values and interests the way her sisters did. She had spent thirty years viewing this as a terrible personal defeat without ever once stopping to realize that her psychological makeup and interests were simply different from the rest of her family's.

Many people report feeling defeated because they've been unable to find a job in a company or organization where they feel valued, or where they can be themselves, or where they're given opportunities to manifest their talents. The result is that they feel disempowered or defensive, or they dread their work. If you feel this way, then my advice is threefold: work on developing new skills and shifting your attitude, and be willing to switch jobs until you find a place that seems to fit. But also beware of getting caught in unrealistic expectations and be mindful of whether there is something in you that needs to change for you to find greater job satisfaction.

Redeeming Personal Defeat

Once a personal defeat is acknowledged and starts to become integrated, you have the possibility of redeeming your failure by harvesting wisdom from it. If you gain insight that makes your life better, then the defeat has served a useful purpose—your suffering was not meaningless. Thus, in helping you be a better and more capable person with a more open heart, the personal defeat is redeemed. You've already had the personal defeat, planted the memory of it in your mind and heart, and it's grown all this time, so what will you reap from it? For instance, you might harvest the insight that you cannot have achievement without also experiencing defeat. Or you might realize the truth that a personal defeat does not define your whole life. Even though your memory of the personal defeat may still be painful or tinged with regret, you now know that you don't have to continue to identify with it. There's nothing to be gained by holding on to wanting your defeat to be different than it was. You may have paid a high price for your defeat, but it's over and you no longer have to keep paying for it.

Self-Soothing Meditation for Hard Times

When a difficult situation or memory arises, your priority is to calm and center yourself. Just notice it and refrain from editorializing. You'll recall that I call this self-soothing. Here is a meditation to help you self-soothe during an emotional emergency.

Go someplace quiet, where you won't be interrupted, and sit comfortably.

Begin by acknowledging what's true. Notice the unpleasant sensations and feelings that are present in your body and mind.

State to yourself, out loud if you can, "This difficulty feels like this." For instance, "Having a broken heart feels like this."

Recognize that in this moment you are suffering, and have compassion for your suffering.

Notice if you are adding to your suffering by criticizing or judging yourself or making up a story about what's happening.

To calm yourself, take a few moments to focus your attention on your breath or one of your senses, such as hearing or seeing, or a part of your body that feels comfortable.

Observe that you are not just this difficulty and that you have other thoughts and bodily sensations. If it helps to calm you, name these thoughts and bodily sensations.

Now notice that these thoughts and bodily sensations are always changing. Seeing that this is true, this feeling of difficulty must also be subject to change and not permanent.

Ask yourself, "Is there something I need to do and can do right now about this difficulty?" If there is, focus on your breath for a few moments and then get up and do it. If there's nothing to be done or you don't know what to do, then just sit there being kind to yourself.

Remind yourself that you can't control all the conditions of your life, but you can choose how you respond to those conditions. Ask yourself, "How do I want to respond to this difficult situation?" Sometimes this question is best asked while taking a meditative walk. You've now moved from your reactive, chaotic mind to being present and clear.

Chapter 20

Practicing Forgiveness and Reconciliation

Not long after the September 11, 2001, terrorist attacks on the United States, I led a meditation group in which we discussed how to forgive the unforgivable. One person talked about how it had taken nearly forty years for her to forgive her father for something heinous, and the moment she did so all the power the story of that act had to rule her life just disappeared. This is the power of forgiveness: it benefits you, empowers you in relation to your loved ones, and even benefits those who have acted harmfully.

Forgiveness may take a long time when what occurred was truly awful. At first you simply can't imagine that forgiveness is possible. You are fixated on the terrible thing that happened; you were helpless, it felt horrible, and it was so wrong. In this fixation you have an unconscious emotional demand that life be fair and just, and you have rage because it is not. You fail to see that life is lawful. All events, pleasant and awful alike, arise out of causes and conditions that are interdependent. Just as good things happen in life, so bad things happen to innocent people because of these conditions. Life, even your life, is at its root impersonal and therefore not to be identified with in such a way that you are imprisoned by the actions of others, no matter how awful or wounding.

There is a poignant story about two Buddhist monks who encounter each other some years after being released from a prison where they had been tortured by their captors. "Have you forgiven them?" asks the first. "I will never forgive them! Never!" replies the second. "Well, I guess they still have you in prison, don't they?" the first says. This story vividly illustrates that forgiveness is about liberating your own feelings and finding meaning in the worst of life's events. You practice forgiveness to be free of the inner violence of your rage, but you do not abandon the pursuit of right action. In fact you gain clear-sightedness that allows you to use skillful means to help bring about sustainable peace.

More than likely the circumstances that you will be challenged to find forgiveness for in your life will be less extreme than the examples I've cited. You may need to forgive a friend who betrayed a secret or failed to support you during a crisis, or a parent who neglected your needs or saddled you with guilt, or a spouse who had an affair, or a colleague who prevented you from getting a promotion. In each of these instances, the reason to forgive is the same: You are the one who is hurt by closing down your heart. When you hold on to anger or revenge, you can't experience the joy that is available in the present moment.

So you practice forgiveness for your own sake, to not be locked in hate, fear, and resentment. Resentment, whether cold fury or smoldering rage, hardens your emotions, narrows your options in responding to life, clouds your judgment, locks you out of experiencing the flow of life, shifts your attention from those who matter to you to those whom you disdain, and deadens your spirit. Why would you choose to live in this manner? It gives those who wronged you an even greater victory than their original act. You can also embrace forgiveness practice as an act of selflessness, something that you can do to stop the seemingly endless cycle of hatred in the world.

Forgiving Isn't an Act of Weakness

The Buddha said, "Hate never yet dispelled hate. Only love dispels hate." By embracing the truth of our interdependency and refusing to participate in this endless cycle of hatred, you can help to heal the wound of the world. Jesus said, "If you love those who love you, what credit is that to you? Even 'sinners' love those who love them. . . . But love your enemies, do good to them, and lend to them without expecting to get anything back. Then your reward will be great."

No one can accuse Jesus or the Buddha of being cowards in the face of injustice; therefore their teachings are about how to hold the difficult in the heart. You have to decide if you share their beliefs, and if so, you practice living in this manner as a reflection of your deepest values. It is a proactive, courageous way to live. Forgiveness does not mean responding passively when you encounter wrong action, for you should always act to stop those who harm others.

We've all either experienced acts of violence that were so horrible they seem unforgivable or know others who have. Maybe it was someone in your family, a friend, your employer, or a stranger. Maybe it resulted in death, or maybe it was the violence of rape, robbery, cheating, or torment. The loss was real, and your life was inevitably shaped by it. You may have lost your childhood, been left with an inability to trust or an unending anger toward others who even slightly offend you or experience problems with intimacy. In all of these situations, the challenge is to not be limited by what happened. You first act to find your own safety; then you act to stop the person from continuing the violations. These outer actions are followed by the hard work of loosening the grip of the experience on your own emotions. Initially it may seem that there is nothing you can do—it happened, it was awful, and your life was ruined. But gradually, after telling your story again and again, you realize it's not the circumstances of the trauma, or even the perpetrator, that's hindering you from moving on. It's you who are clinging to the trauma in shock and hurt. You understand that as long as you continue to do so, like the monk who was still imprisoned by his torturer, you will never be free, and so you begin the painful inner work.

Anger's False Promise

Forgiveness is so difficult to achieve because whatever has occasioned the need for forgiveness has caused the mind to be clouded by pain, loss, and confusion. The natural response to pain is to stamp out the source and make the pain go away. When there is trauma, this response tends to be locked in: feelings of loss play over and over again, arising from wishing things to be different. This is compounded by survivor's guilt, a false sense that one "should have known," which arises in hindsight, and by the need to make loss seem rational by assigning the blame and acting out retribution. Confusion comes from the dramatic change caused by trauma: things were one way; now they are another—what is one to do? These emotions are spontaneous and natural, but by practicing mindfulness you can avoid identifying with them. The mind will become clouded over and over again; many times you will not even notice that there is any other choice. But eventually you will remember your commitment not to live in anger, and you will act to align yourself with your true values.

When pain, loss, and confusion cloud the mind, they can be worked with directly. Far more difficult are the emotions that block the mind in a more permanent fashion, such as anger, lust for revenge, hatred, and attachment to these emotions, which causes you to become identified with them. This negative identification is static in nature, so you tend to stay the same, not to heal, and not to look forward but look back. Tragically, you become one with anger and end up its servant. It is a reactive rather than a proactive manner of living, one based in doing to another, not in being with yourself. It implies a false promise of peace: "If only you could make them pay!"

Refusing to forgive leads to other forms of darkness as well. First there is the lowest-common-denominator effect, in which the victim feels justified in saying, "If my son lost his life, then my enemy should lose his." This is one of the roots of escalating conflict and only leads to a downward spiral in which each party loses more of what he has.

There is also the darkness that results from using hatred or anger as a substitute emotion when you cannot stay fully present in your loss, fear, and vulnerability. And finally there are cases when the refusal to forgive continues because the real resentment is against whatever God or life itself. Unable to be angry with God or life directly, one remains stuck, fixated on the immediate enemy.

Rage versus Outrage

With the freedom that comes from forgiveness, you are motivated to work not for retribution, but for fairness. You understand that only in a just and fair world can there ever be peace and safety. Power alone, as events have shown, always has a weakness that in time reveals itself. Horrible events happen because of conditions; therefore once you change the conditions, you greatly reduce the chances of horrible things happening.

When there is a sense of fairness, one also receives much more cooperation in putting an end to horrible things. Think of it as the difference between rage and outrage. They both have determination and passion and lead to action, but rage is narrow, short term, and blinded by fury, while outrage is broad, clear, steady, and committed to a sustainable solution. With forgiveness comes sympathy for life's uncertainty and determination to be there for others when they experience loss and to help in any way possible. If one has embraced the intent to practice forgiveness, then one is willing to share one's own story and allow others to share theirs in a mutual search for a way out of the clutches of anger and rage.

Forgiveness is an intention with which to approach life. The Bible says, "Forgive, and you shall be forgiven." Know full well that you, like everyone else, have to account for your own acts of greed, hatred, and delusion, many of which you have no awareness of at present. This is the humility of the human condition. It is the basis for understanding that the best you can do is to seek to know what's true, to be willing to examine and learn about yourself from your own actions and the actions of others, and to act with kindness and fairness to all, even the enemy.

Forgiveness has additional challenges when it involves your community or country. You may feel as though you are being disloyal to others or betraying the victims. You may experience great comfort and a sense of belonging through sharing in the anger of the larger community and not want to lose that feeling. You may feel secure in the energy of the community's rage and feel more frightened when you start to walk your own path.

You may question, "Who am I to follow my own path?" Each of these emotions is understandable, and maybe you are not ready to embrace the act of forgiving. But remember this: *forgiveness is inclusive*. It includes forgiving those who cannot let loose of their anger in your community, and it even means forgiving those who commit misguided acts of revenge against innocent people. By practicing forgiveness you are not trying to separate but to include, without forsaking discernment or abandoning your commitment to law, safety, and fairness for all.

Forgiveness Practice

It is possible to cultivate forgiveness through meditation. Some Western Buddhist meditation teachers begin loving-kindness practice with a three-part forgiveness practice asking forgiveness of all those you may have harmed through thoughts, words, or actions. You then offer forgiveness for any harm others have caused you through their thoughts, words, and actions, as best you are able. Finally, you offer forgiveness to yourself for any harm you have done to yourself.

These phrases are repeated a number of times, then you move on to loving-kindness practice, having cultivated the intention to remove the reactions that cloud the mind and the emotions that block the heart. Your responsibility is for your intention; you are practicing clarifying and purifying the intention to be a forgiving person, no matter how difficult the circumstance.

Many times your actual emotional experience will be anger, rage, fear, and grief—anything but forgiveness. This is why it's called forgiveness practice. *Webster's* provides a second definition of *forgive*: "To give up claim to requital from or retribution upon an offender." This too offers the possibility of insight. When a horrible act is committed, there is understandably a clamor for justice, and it often carries with it a sense of entitlement. Every society throughout history has evolved a way to mete out justice, whether through banishment, loss of privilege, shame, isolation, physical punishment, forced compensation, or execution. Justice is a symbolic ritual with two purposes: to stop the behavior from occurring again and to restore the harmony that was disrupted by the violent act.

When a life has been lost or great physical or mental damage done, there is no going back; there is only going forward. If you hold on to a personal claim because of what you lost, you assume the identity of the victim. It may seem right and proper, but oftentimes it is just another form of self-imprisonment. In the parable of the mustard seed, a distraught mother comes to the Buddha with her dead child in her arms, pleading with him to bring her child back to life. The Buddha says he will do so if she can bring him a mustard seed from a household that has not known death. The woman frantically goes from house to house, asking if they have not known death, until finally she realizes that all households have known death, and she is able to accept that great loss is part of life.

When you suffer a great loss, you may rightly seek redress. However, justice, which is rooted in love, compassion, and harmony, is not the same thing as revenge, which is rooted in anger, hatred, and ill will. When you are possessed by thoughts of revenge, you have become the very mind state that you deplored in your aggressor. It can lead to deluded thinking in which you feel that your grief and loss entitle you to abuse someone else. From the perspective of the inner life, feelings of revenge, hatred, and ill will arise out of aversion and delusion, and they are degrading to your life, a form of self-affliction that is the opposite of being loving to yourself and honoring someone whose death you mourn.

To meet hatred and loss with love and a generous heart is the most difficult practice imaginable. Sometimes I hesitate to teach it, for I have my own struggles with anger and hardening of the heart as a reaction to terrible and unjust acts. Yet what is the purpose of a practice if you are not going to use it in life's difficult moments? It requires humility to surrender to the mystery of life and its unpredictability. It requires an equal amount of courage to face life's losses and be willing to say, "This too is life," and bear it as you find it, even while doing everything in your power to change it into a gentler, safer experience.

The practice of forgiveness along with compassion and love is the most powerful ground you can prepare for the future well-being of your children. If they see you violent in thoughts, words, and actions, they will learn violence as a reaction, no matter what you tell them. But if they see you meet hate with love, they will manifest this as adults. To repeat the Buddha, "Hate never yet dispelled hate; only love dispels hate."

When Forgiveness Isn't Possible, Practice Reconciliation

At present you may not be able to find forgiveness because you are too emotionally raw or fearful. If this is your situation, then practicing *reconciliation* can help bring about peace in your mind, which will allow your heart to soften.

To reconcile means to restore to compatibility or harmony, as well as to restore the sacred. The word is also used to mean "to make consistent or congruous"—for example, to reconcile your ideals with reality. When you practice reconciliation, you are reconciling yourself to the truth that in the present moment there is enmity between you and another. Rather than allowing your heart to become closed to the other, you are seeking to align the mind and heart to accept that person *just as they are.*

There is a tremendous cost to your well-being when you shut your heart to others. On the most practical level, being shut down by anger or hate is not an effective position for working toward change. It breeds feelings of despair, victimhood, and what is called *learned helplessness.*

Refusing to reconcile to the way things are also means that you are draining your energy in a hopeless demand that what has already happened not be true. One meditation teacher put it this way: "Do not hope for a better past."

Finally, closing your heart to others in an attempt to avoid admitting to yourself that you, like all other humans, are capable of unskillful behavior prevents you from feeling your own emotions. Reconciliation practice is the aligning and softening of the heart *to be reconciled with the present moment just as it is.* It doesn't involve resignation or defeat. It is a way to embrace the entirety of your experience, with nothing left out, not even the things you think you can't live with. When you don't separate yourself from parts of your experience, you have better access both to your wisdom and to your deepest values, and therefore your actions tend to be more skillful.

To experience reconciliation you must acknowledge the truth of your estrangement from the other person. A successful reconciliation is not contingent on becoming best friends with the person. Rather the intention to be reconciled is the wish to be connected to your deepest intentions in the present moment despite your hostility or suffering and to find harmony within any situation, even the most painful. This does not mean that you have to approve of what is unskillful or to forsake passionately advocating what you believe to be right. This is the understanding reflected by the Dalai Lama when he refers to the Chinese as "my friends, the enemy."

Accept the Truth

One of my students had been frozen in anger for many months, unable to deal with the practicalities of her divorce; she was struggling to forgive her husband even while he continued a pattern of hurtful actions. She finally realized that she was stuck because of her unrecognized demand that he change. Through reconciliation practice, she was able to accept him as he was and negotiate a parting that minimized the turmoil for their young child. A second student, to his own amazement, reconnected with his alienated wife once he reconciled himself to certain difficulties in her personality. Another person was able to let go of the outrage he had long held toward his abusive father, and another found that an intolerable supervisor at work could in fact be tolerated, if not respected.

In none of these instances did the student report strong feelings of compassion or loving-kindness for the other person. Instead each experienced the release of inner tension that had been blocking an acceptance of the truth of how things were. Once the truth of the moment had been accepted, each of their situations could be worked with in a manner that brought inner peace and at times outright resolution. They were able to be reconciled whether or not their antagonist was participating in the process, and it felt great!

Reconciliation is not the end point of the practice. It is a beginning, a place from which to continue to free your heart. Through reconciliation, you gain momentum toward loving-kindness—an unconditional well-wishing that flows freely from the unencumbered heart, *independent of conditions.*

The Dalai Lama emanates such a feeling. The woman who was finally able to divorce her husband is only now able to experience moments of loving-kindness toward him as another being who, as the Buddha taught, "just wishes to be happy." Likewise, the student with the difficult boss reports that on some occasions when his boss is acting out compassion arises in him for such a tormented soul. Reconciliation provides the *acknowledgment and alignment* that allow for such promptings of the heart to emerge.

One man reported success in practicing reconciliation toward political leaders he found contemptible. He imagined his views and feelings as constituting one circle of existence, and the values and unskillful actions of the politicians to be a separate circle. Through reconciliation he came to realize there was a third, larger circle of existence containing both smaller circles. This understanding allowed him to find some harmony with people he'd previously held in contempt. I sometimes refer to this larger circle as the *ground of reconciliation*. By resting in this place, we can avoid inhabiting the small circle of a separate identity.

Reconciliation practice can also be brought into the larger community. One long-term *vipassanā* practitioner in Arizona has formed an organization of fellow lawyers who are committed to the practice of being reconciled. Two members of this group agreed to represent divorcing spouses in settlement talks, with the understanding that if the parties couldn't reconcile their child-custody and material differences out of court, then both lawyers would resign. In North Carolina, a pastor has started a truth-and-reconciliation commission modeled on the one in South Africa, in an effort to reconcile community differences around Ku Klux Klan actions in earlier decades.

The Joy of Having a Wise Heart

I realize that the topics of forgiveness and reconciliation may be upsetting to you and that you may react with an attitude of angry dismissal, thinking that I am being naive or unreal or worse. You will not be the first to reach this conclusion. But experience has shown me that however great your suffering, *if you can consciously bear it without turning to hatred or bitterness, you will experience greater peace of mind than you have ever known.* You will have the capacity to accept life as it is, even as you work passionately to create a meaningful, authentic life that's aligned with your values. You will be able to live an inclusive life, without the need to categorize or shut anyone out of your heart, even the person who can't be trusted or must be guarded against. When you are willing to accept and forgive life for being the mixed experience of suffering and joy that it is, you've developed what is called a *wise heart*. You then have the clarity of mind that allows you to bear your suffering and the suffering of those you care for, to make uncomfortable but necessary compromises, to let go of your expectations, and to accept the way things are without losing your ability to love and care.

Practices for Forgiveness and Reconciliation

Find a quiet place and sit comfortably. Have the forgiveness or reconciliation practice phrases given here in front of you the first few times you try these practices; eventually they will be etched in your memory. Repeating the phrases at a steady pace builds your concentration and intention.

You may feel that you can't possibly forgive, but it is your intention to forgive that you are cultivating in forgiveness practice. The results come in their own time. By simply having the intention to forgive, you are opening your heart to the possibility. If only one of the three forgiveness phrases seems relevant at a given time, just repeat it over and over again.

Some people practice only the first half of the reconciliation meditation, which has to do with family and relationships, and others only practice the second half, which has to do with being in the greater community. Say each phrase three times as you go through the practice. When you face a difficult situation that corresponds to a specific phrase, it may be useful to simply repeat that phrase over and over. Sometimes strong emotions arise and what you feel is anything but acceptance and reconciliation. Don't be discouraged: this is an ideal time to incline your heart to your deepest values.

Forgiveness Practice

For any harm I may have caused others knowingly or unknowingly through my thoughts, words, or actions, I ask their forgiveness.

For any harm others may have caused me knowingly or unknowingly through their thoughts, words, and actions, I forgive them as best I am able.

For any harm I may have caused myself knowingly or unknowingly through my thoughts, words, and actions, I forgive myself as best I am able.

Reconciliation Practice

May all fathers and daughters be reconciled.

May all mothers and sons be reconciled.

May all mothers and daughters be reconciled.

May all fathers and sons be reconciled.

May all brothers and sisters, sisters and sisters, and brothers and brothers be reconciled.

May all mothers and fathers be reconciled.

May all husbands and wives, lovers, and partners be reconciled.

May all friends and enemies be reconciled.

May all teachers and students be reconciled.

May all communities and their members be reconciled.

May all countries and their citizens be reconciled.

May all warring nations be reconciled.

May all practitioners of religions be reconciled.

May all people everywhere be reconciled.

May all people and this earth be reconciled.

Epilogue: What Next?

For the guidance I promised at the beginning of this book to be complete, I ask that you do one more thing: please reread chapter 2, "Getting to Know the Real You." Answering, once again, the questions about how you form identity that are raised in that chapter should provide you with a strong sense of completion in your understanding, and it will point the way to where you go from here.

While writing this book, I debated at length whether to put the chapter on identity at the beginning or at the end. The truth is that gaining greater clarity about who you really are and what truly matters to you constitutes both a beginning and an ending in your endeavor to find freedom from chaos. Maybe I should have just repeated chapter 2 at the end of the book without any explanation, for it naturally fits in both places!

In Your End Is Your Beginning

Rereading chapter 2 is consistent with the Buddhist approach to developing wisdom. When you read the second chapter once more, you'll discover that you've gained deeper insight about the knowledge that is being presented and how it applies to your life. In Buddhism this insight is called *right* or *wise understanding*, and at every stage of your inner development you both begin and end with wise understanding. For instance, it was your right understanding of the chaos in your mind that motivated you to read this book in the first place. Now you are at the end of this phase of your exploration, and your level of right understanding is more complete, and you are wiser than when you started. Both levels of understanding—the one with which you started and the one you now possess—are equally valuable because you could not have reached this deeper level of understanding if you did not have the initial one.

Why does this distinction that I'm making between levels of right understanding matter? It's important because beginnings and endings are transition points in your life, and how you enact them greatly influences the results. When you end a relationship or a job, for example, you are simultaneously at the threshold of a new begin-ning. The intention and quality of attention with which you begin something new will greatly influence how it ends. Likewise, the mindfulness with which you end something affects how the new beginning will unfold. Thus the ending that is occurring now as you finish reading this book is also a new beginning in your journey toward self-understanding. This paradoxical learning pattern allows understanding to develop into liberating insights about the truth of the way things are and how to live more skillfully.

Living from Clarity

As you gain clarity, you will discover that you have a new capacity for a more harmonious relationship to life. But to fully realize this insight, you must begin to apply it in your daily life. The most effective place to start is with understanding how misconceptions about your iden-tity trap you in unhappiness (as described in chapter 2).

Life is undeniably stressful, uncertain, and dissatisfying at times, as well as physically and emotionally painful. But through wise understanding, you gain the insight that much of your suffering is caused by your mistaken views about who you are, which create misperceptions about what will bring you happiness. This in turn leads you to cling fiercely to the very things that are causing you so much suffering! But finally, one day, you gain the clarity to see how you create so much of your own suffering. Motivated by this insight, you simply stop repeating the patterns, at least in some areas of your life.

After Clarity, Then What?

Certain questions may emerge when you cease to be a puppet being pulled one way or the other by the strings of desire and aversion, among them: "What comes after clarity?" "Now that I'm somewhat self-contained and internally motivated, what are my goals?" "What is my basis for making choices in life when I am no longer motivated by the immediate needs of my ego?" "How do I decide what to do with my time once I have taken care of my basic needs?" These are appropriate questions at this time—they challenge you to continue your practice of mindfulness and to reflect on your intentions so that you can realize an even deeper understanding of what matters in life. These questions are able to arise now only because you have achieved enough clarity to be aware they even exist.

Don't Miss the Moment of Realizing the Imaginative Possible

In the introduction to this book, I referred to realizing the imaginative possible, the moment when you suddenly have the confidence that achieving a skill or developing a capacity is a reality. You know you are capable of changing your inner experience of life no matter what the outer conditions are.

If you continue with the mindfulness practices I have described in this book, your moment of realizing the imaginative possible will happen. (It may have already occurred for you; if so, you need to acknowledge it for your development to continue.) All aspects of your life will then become opportunities for you to seek clarity about what genuinely matters and to speak and act accordingly. The ease in life you will discover as you gain clarity will make the effort and occasional discomfort involved in these practices worthwhile.

A moment of realizing the imaginative possible is also both an ending and a beginning. It is the end result of your hard work, and it is a new beginning because for the imaginative possible to manifest in your life, you must be committed to continuing to develop your capacity for clarity. One surprising benefit of making this commitment is that even the mundane aspects of life take on new dimensions of meaning. The reason this happens is that you are now placing at least as much emphasis on your internal experience as your external one.

T. S. Eliot and Clarifying Intention

The poet T. S. Eliot, who was a devout Anglican Christian, examined this question of what you do once you find clarity in his *Four Quartets*. His inquiries and answers had a profound impact on my own development and influenced what I've written here. In *Four Quartets*, Eliot asks what gives life meaning and unity despite the chaos that's created by continual change. In his answers he draws not only on Christian teachings but also on Buddhism, Hinduism, and ancient Greek philosophy.

In the first of the book's four poems, "Burnt Norton," Eliot says that your inner stillness is the center of the universe: "At the still point of the turning world . . . there the dance is." When you can connect with that stillness, you gain a sense of clarity and joy that is beyond the happiness that can be found in the struggle to achieve gain and avoid loss that takes place in ordinary time and perception. (Sometimes you just happen to stumble into this stillness, but it can be cultivated through certain meditation and contemplative prayer practices.) In the second poem, "The Dry Salvages," Eliot explains that only in those moments when you are fully present can you make a difference in the life of another or in your own: "on whatever . . . the mind of a man may be intent . . . that is the one action . . . which shall fructify in the lives of others."

In the third poem, "East Coker," Eliot states that you can't rely on perceptions that do not come from actual experience; therefore you must give up your fixed views and "go by a way which is the way of ignorance." These reflections and the many other insights Eliot offers create the framework in which he then presents his understanding of how to continue to live life once you gain some amount of clarity.

Finally, in "Little Gidding," the last of the poems, Eliot eloquently addresses the question of how we come to terms with life just as it is. He does so by borrowing a quote from Dame Julian of Norwich, a fourteenth-century Christian mystic: "All shall be well and all manner of thing shall be well," to which he adds this directive:

> *By the purification of the motive*
> *In the ground of our beseeching.*

His answer is that well-being comes from continually clarifying and purifying your intention, which he calls "the motive." As you do, you intuitively know that "all manner of thing shall be well," even those things that you despise about life.

For Eliot, intention is the key to well-being because it is the "ground" from which all wanting arises. As you gain more clarity about how things truly are, your intentions naturally become less distorted by greed and aversion, and your sense of well-being grows proportionally.

Eliot's answer is strikingly similar to what the Buddha taught. I have found no better answer in all my years of exploration. By opening to the joy and suffering of this world and meeting them both with mindfulness and compassion, you gain still further clarity as to your intention.

Clarity has a purifying effect on your intentions and therefore your actions. Once you gain the clarity to see that suffering occurs when you have ill will and that chaos arises in your mind when it is obsessed with wanting, you simply cease your delusional behavior. Your wanting (which Eliot and Dame Julian call "beseeching") doesn't suddenly disappear, but instead of arising out of the chaos of your reactive mind states, your desires are purified by your intention.

I have spent decades learning how to live out the "purification of the motive" in daily life, and I am still very much a work in progress. Therefore don't expect it to manifest in your life immediately. However, Eliot's words hint at what's possible for you through continual practice—that the purification of the motive will bring "a further union, a deeper communion" with what is mysterious in life. We slowly connect with this mystery through living from the clarity of our deepest intention.

Now please go back and reread chapter 2, for in this ending is your beginning.

ONLINE RESOURCES

Visit emotionalchaostoclarity.com

Reading this book is an important first step toward developing a responsive mind; however, it takes patience and persistence to retrain the mind. Therefore I've created a Web site, emotionalchaos toclarity.com, to provide ongoing support to you in your intention to live more skillfully. Some of the features you'll find on the Web site include:

Working with Difficult Emotions Video

In this fifteen-minute video, I talk about how to use the skills you've learned in this book to work through specific emotional challenges, such as anger, envy, and frustration.

Emotional Chaos to Clarity Free Weekly E-teaching

Receive a visually inspiring teaching based on *Emotional Chaos to Clarity* in your e-mail in-box each week for a year. Each teaching contains a key passage from the book with questions for further reflection and self-study. These weekly e-mails will help you remember your intentions and encourage you to practice living skillfully.

Emotional Chaos to Clarity Study Guide

If you're interested in reading *Emotional Chaos to Clarity* in a book group, want to start a book study group, or simply want to study the book in more depth on your own, sign up to receive free access to this online study guide, which offers suggestions for structuring your approach to reading the book.

Phillip Moffitt's Teaching Schedule

In addition to leading meditation retreats at Spirit Rock Insight Meditation Center and other *vipassanā* centers around the country, I also lead a weekly meditation group, Marin Sangha, in San Rafael, California. You can find my teaching schedule on emotionalchaostoclarity .com, as well as on my teaching Web site, dharmawisdom.org.

Other Resources Available on emotionalchaostoclarity.com

- Listen to talks and read articles about mindfulness, intention, and living skillfully.
- Learn where to go on a meditation retreat.
- Find other books that can help you in your journey from emotional chaos to clarity.
- Find out more about Buddhism and mindfulness meditation.

Index